CONTRAFLOW

FROM NEW ORLEANS TO HOUSTON
A story of leadership witnessed after Hurricane Katrina

STELLAR
COMMUNICATIONS
HOUSTON

More Praise for Contraflow

"Bill Herrington's moving account of Katrina reminded me of those challenging days when so many responded so generously to the needs of friends they had yet to meet."

— *Daniel K. Lahart,*
SJ, President, Strake Jesuit College Preparatory

"Contraflow tells accurately how New Orleanians were impacted after Hurricane Katrina."

— *Newell Normand,*
Sheriff of Jefferson Parish, Louisiana

"When Hurricane Katrina hit New Orleans, leaders were beginning to collaborate in new and exciting ways. Bill Herrington describes how the storm affected the region—and how New Orleanians regained their hope."

— *Mary Landrieu,*
former senator of Louisiana

"The book is an authentic story of one family's recovery in the aftermath of Katrina. It is filled with adventure, compassion, community service, humor and love. It is a book that every New Orleanian and Houstonian who struggled through Katrina will certainly enjoy."

— *James Meza, Jr.,*
former superintendent of Jefferson Parish public schools

"Bill Herrington offers an engaging and honest first-person account of how Hurricane Katrina impacted New Orleanians of all types in all walks of life and how Houstonians, seeing people in need, stepped up to help them."

– Debbie Harwell,
Ph.D., Managing Editor, Houston History,
Center for Public History, University of Houston

"Katrina was more than incessant battering wind, driving rain, and rising water. Contraflow weaves in the horrendous with the tears of joy and accomplishments that no one could have foreseen or yearned for. Years from now, many will research and detail events and relevant facts of those dreadful days, weeks, and months. This chronicle includes facts as well as insight into the souls and minds of some real people that actually lived and endured and, in many ways, beat Katrina."

– Randy Howard,
former board member and commercial head of Hibernia
National Bank

CONTRAFLOW: FROM NEW ORLEANS TO HOUSTON
A STORY OF LEADERSHIP WITNESSED AFTER HURRICANE KATRINA

Paperback 978-0-9976496-2-8
Hardcover 978-0-9976496-3-5
E-book 978-0-9976496-4-2

Stellar Communications Houston
www.stellarwriter.com
281.804.7089

Written with Ramon A. Vargas
Editing and Preparation for publication by Ella Hearrean Ritchie
Cover design and formatting by Jamie Tipton

Dedicated to the 60,000 volunteers in Houston, Texas, who helped administer the largest evacuation operation of a U.S. city in American history, especially the "men for others" at Strake Jesuit College Preparatory.

CONTENTS

Acknowledgements

There are many people who helped me make this book a reality, but I wanted to take a brief minute and specifically highlight these few.

Russ Hoadley, thank you for writing the account about Hibernia's experience during Katrina and acknowledging the bank's efforts. For those interested, Russ' account, "A Beacon of Hope: Hibernia Bank's Recovery from Hurricane Katrina," is well worth a read, and it can be found online at www.hiberniakatrina.com.

The Center for Public History at the University of Houston, thank you for so carefully preserving the account of Hurricane Katrina in *Houston History's* "Houston's Helping Hand: Remembering Katrina," which is the source of much of chapter seven in this book. Your initiative helps Houstonians develop a respectful understanding of others' experiences as well as the history of Houston.

Dianne and Jimmy Moss, my dear sister and brother-in-law: Thank you for taking us in after Katrina. And Jimmy, thank you for helping me with the difficult work of cleaning our home after Katrina.

And last but certainly not least, Ella Hearrean Ritchie and Ramon Antonio Vargas, thank you for helping me get this story ready that I'd been pondering writing for the better part of a decade. Ella is a Houston-based publisher whose Cajun family had dealt with flooding and FEMA trailers after the storm. Ramon Vargas has been a resident of the New Orleans area his whole life and has been working as a journalist there since 2006.

Preface

Along the coast of the Gulf of Mexico, the term "contraflow" is well known to local residents. It is a term synonymous with an evacuation due to an approaching hurricane.

Contraflow refers to the reversal of incoming traffic lanes on major highways during times of emergency to improve the flow of cars. In contraflow, the number of outbound lanes is doubled during evacuations, and all incoming cars are blocked until the order to leave town is lifted.

But to me, contraflow is about more than traffic logistics. It is an ominous expression that will always remind me how fragile life is and how a peaceful existence can be unexpectedly and abruptly reversed.

This is the true story of the lives of people, businesses, and entire cities that were temporarily reversed and permanently altered by Hurricane Katrina, one of the most catastrophic storms on record. On August 29, 2005, the tropical storm breached the hurricane protection surge system in New Orleans, flooding eighty percent of the city and killing approximately 1,400 people. It is considered the worst civil engineering disaster in the history of the United States.

Although several worthy books have been written about Hurricane Katrina, I wanted to tell this particular story for three reasons.

First, this is the story of leadership and compassion on a scale I had never seen before and may never have the occasion to witness again. The magnitude of the devastation and the suffering in New Orleans perhaps overshadowed the extensive humanitarian response, particularly in Houston. But the truth that emerged from Katrina is that unexpected disasters can reveal the best in people. I witnessed this truth in some of the civic, corporate, and community leaders who stepped up to help families and businesses recover when others did not, even if doing so invited criticism from some quarters. In Houston, three of the best people who call that city home come to mind: Former Harris County Judge Robert Eckels, former Houston Mayor Bill White, and Father Dan Lahart of Strake Jesuit. Their leadership was both unanticipated and underreported, so this story is a tribute to them so that their actions can be celebrated and can serve as a guide in future catastrophes.

Second, this is the story of the impact of the storm on the entire community. The lives of New Orleanians were starting to look up prior to the storm, slowly but steadily recovering from the 1980s oil bust and the unsuccessful 1984 New Orleans World's Fair. A cross-section of regional New Orleans insiders were collaborating, perhaps as never before, to reverse the declining trends in economic development, education, and political leadership. These efforts seemed to be working, even resulting in the relocation of the NBA's Charlotte Hornets to New Orleans in 2002.

But when Hurricane Katrina struck, it forever changed the lives of many New Orleanians. We were all suddenly thrust into a new, non-exclusive class of people who were vulnerable in ways we had never even imagined. The media focused primarily on the poor. But our members were rich and poor, young and old, of all skin colors, ethnicities, and religions—every economic and social sector of the community. We shared overwhelming losses in the storm, including homes, possessions, schools, churches, and workplaces. To make a tragic situation even worse, looters took advantage of many residents who had been displaced to other states and cities throughout the country.

The victims who were most deeply affected lost their family members to the storm. Less obvious was the impact felt by families who lost their sense of community after the storm. Churches, sports teams, playgrounds, businesses and, perhaps most importantly, schools, all shut down, both temporarily and permanently. For many storm victims, those institutions formed a network of support throughout the city that was lost in Katrina's aftermath. Katrina's wind and waves destroyed this network, leaving families stranded and searching for a place to belong. That sense of camaraderie, of family, is one of the most important aspects of small communities like New Orleans.

Finally, this is the story of the strong institutions that serve as the glue for good communities. I became intimately aware of how schools, social service organizations, religious organizations, and nonprofits are foundational to helping people recover from crises. Some families were lucky, like mine, and I share our journey in recognition of the people and institutions who served as temporary pillars in our life. But some people who did not have resources will never fully recover, particularly displaced children who did not have good academic options after the disaster. Their lack of resources re-traumatized these victims during an already challenging time in their life. For this reason, a good portion of this story is dedicated to the realization of the importance of education.

Bill Herrington

PART ONE

COUNTDOWN TO DESTRUCTION

CHAPTER 1

THREE DAYS BEFORE THE STORM

Friday, August 26, 2005

9:30 a.m.

Right away, it was obvious that something was wrong.

I had just arrived at the administration building of the newly renovated Medard H. Nelson Charter School, mentally reviewing my talking points before the press conference that would be held for its grand re-opening.

The elementary school was located at 3121 St. Bernard Avenue in the central part of New Orleans near the intersection of St. Bernard Avenue and Interstate 610. The campus was inconspicuous and similar to many other typical school buildings with a cream-colored brick exterior, with its name highlighted in bright orange lettering on the front wall.

But it wasn't the plain exterior that excited me. It was what was going on inside. I adjusted my tie and patted the front pocket of one of my favorite suits with a satisfied smile.

Inside the pocket was a neatly tucked cashier's check that I would be presenting to the school on behalf of Hibernia National Bank, the largest bank headquartered in the state of Louisiana. I had worked for the bank for nearly twenty years and I was looking forward to one of the most rewarding community involvement presentations with which I've ever been involved. The bank had approved its largest donation ever of $250,000 for the sponsorship of the Medard Nelson Charter School in support of a bold new charter school education initiative. A cross section of the city's elite would be there, including Louisiana Senator Mary Landrieu, some city council members, the University of New Orleans (UNO) Education Dean Jim Meza, and UNO President Tim Ryan.

But as soon as I entered the schoolroom, I stopped abruptly. People were scurrying around, looking anxious and nervous. Across the room, Senator Landrieu was listening intently to something that one of her aides was telling her. The Senator looked concerned.

A few moments later, one of the school administrators walked to the front and asked for everyone's attention.

"Ladies and gentlemen," the administrator said, clearing her throat, "thank you all for coming. Unfortunately, Mother Nature has caused us to change our plans. Mayor Ray Nagin has just ordered a voluntary evacuation due to the threat of Tropical Storm Katrina. Again, thank you for coming, but the news conference has been canceled, as we need to prepare for evacuation."

And just like that, my big day turned into a big dud.

I couldn't believe it. Weeks of planning had gone into this press conference, but within minutes, the television cameraman and newspaper reporters were packed up and streaming out of the room and back into the heat and humidity of a typical August morning in New Orleans.

But my disappointment in this moment was no match for what was coming. I didn't know that in a few days, I would witness one of most devastating events in American history, one that would change the lives of everyone in and around New Orleans. Young, old, rich, poor—none of us were exempt from the force that would pummel our city.

Even more life-changing would be the unanticipated compassion and leadership that would emerge from the wreckage. I was about to experience humanitarian efforts unlike anything I had ever witnessed before.

But I didn't know any of that this morning. Feeling dejected, I followed the group out of the building and trudged back to my car, unaware of what was in store. I sighed, readjusted my tie, and reflected on the events that had led to the press meeting.

A History of Community Activism[1]

The bank I worked for had developed a reputation for helping people in the community almost as soon as it had been established on Camp Street as Hibernia Bank & Trust Company on April 30, 1870, when a dozen Irishmen held the first meeting of the board of directors. They had chosen the name "Hibernia" in honor of the land of their ancient Roman ancestors.

The bank was born in a city that was much different than the New Orleans we know today. At that time, New Orleans had a population of about 170,000 people, forty percent of whom were foreign-born, and 24,000 of whom were Irish, according to a Hibernia annual shareholder's report from 1994.

But its passion for the community was evident from the beginning. One example was the devotion of "Hibernians" to selling war bonds. And in addition to providing assistance during natural disasters, Hibernia supported two World's Fairs a century apart—in 1884 and again in 1984—and have supported hundreds of nonprofits over the years.

---

[1] Some of the information in this section was derived from Hibernia Corporation's *1994 Annual Report*.

In 1921, the bank constructed a building for its headquarters that was recognized as an architectural and engineering marvel, sparking a building boom in New Orleans. The building would remain New Orleans' tallest building until 1964. The building—especially its cupola, a shining tower that was illuminated at night—was hailed as a beacon of commerce and a symbol of a fast-growing economy.

But the bank didn't stop there in making a mark. In 1933, Hibernia President Rudolph Hecht arranged the federal financing for the first bridge over the Mississippi River in the New Orleans area, the Huey P. Long Bridge.

Almost sixty years later, in 1992, Hibernia recruited Steve Hansel to the bank after posting sizeable losses during a real estate crisis. Hansel quickly recapitalized the company, administering an ambitious acquisition program of buying smaller community banks around the state. Under this vision, Hibernia became the largest bank to be headquartered in the state of Louisiana as well as one of the largest in the southeastern United States.

It was during this time that I managed commercial banking in New Orleans for Hibernia National Bank. I appreciated the fact that my role at Hibernia afforded me an inside view of the progress the region was making. My wife Frances, a teacher, and I enjoyed participating in the economic development and educational aspects of New Orleans along with many others in the bank and the community who shared a similar passion for improving the city.

A Reform Agenda Takes Hold

The charter school network was spearheaded by Jim Meza, the UNO dean of education who initially struck me as a friendly, affable, and mild-mannered guy. Jim was affable, all right, but his aggressive approach with prospective sponsors would later tell me that he was anything but mild-mannered. His determination was evidence of a shift in the attitude around New Orleans. He embodied how fed up the business community was with the languishing economy and poor schools. Leslie Jacobs, a businesswoman then serving on the Board of Elementary and Secondary Education (BESE), proposed a statewide recovery school district that could take control of individual failing schools. The measure required a constitutional amendment before it was implemented, and voters ratified it that year.

Thanks to the pervasive attitude toward education throughout Louisiana and the dogged perseverance of Jim, Hibernia ultimately approved a large contribution that supported the University of New Orleans in its takeover of a chronically failing Orleans parish school and establishment of a charter school under the new legislation that Leslie Jacobs had secured. Pierre A. Capdau Charter School would be operated under the corporate umbrella of the New Beginnings Foundation, a non-profit charter school governing board with duties and responsibilities similar to a local school board. Its three founding board members were Tim Ryan, the UNO chancellor; Meza, his dean of education; and me.

Capdau opened in August 2004 in the 4600 block of Canal Street. The new charter school progressed steadily in its first year, and Hibernia was pleased that it had made a charitable investment in something that made such a difference.

Bolstered by the success, Jim pursued more schools for the New Beginnings Foundation. When he heard my supportive comments of charter schools over a couple of beers at a Hornets basketball game, he wasted no time in calling me the next day to remind me of my comments and to say that he was counting on Hibernia for financial support.

I was caught off guard at how boldly Jim had expressed

his expectations so I hedged a bit, but Jim remained unfazed. I soon recognized that the affable Jim Meza was also a bulldog who cajoled, schmoozed, and sometimes threatened until he got the support he needed—including that of the bank—to start his charter school network. Jim had served as a colonel in the Louisiana National Guard, and he had likely encountered far stronger resistance than I could offer. Thanks to his efforts, he drummed up support from Hibernia for his charter school network.

The Press Conference that Never Happened

The grand opening of the second charter school was planned on the morning of August 26, 2005. Meza had presented the second plan to the bank, and Hibernia had approved a $250,000 grant toward the takeover of the Medard H. Nelson Elementary School in New Orleans.

I was looking forward to presenting Hibernia's largest ever donation to the school and giving a speech to the media. U.S. Senator Mary Landrieu had supported the charter school initiative, and she would be there as well. On the morning before the press conference, I joined my wife downstairs for coffee and told her all about the exciting events that were planned that day.

"That's great," she said, beaming at me over the brim of her coffee cup. She knew how invested I'd become in the charter school movement in New Orleans.

Inflated, I'd continued, "Yeah, it's a pretty big deal. The media will be there, and I'll probably have to make a speech about the history of the UNO charter school network and how it got started and all. Mary and I will probably both have to say a few words and get interviewed on television."

Frances raised her eyebrows at the mention of the

senator's first name. "Mary?" she asked. "So, you're on a first name basis with Senator Landrieu now?"

I couldn't tell if my wife was mocking me for suggesting a level of familiarity with another woman or for being too excited, so I backtracked and said, "Oh, you know what I mean. It just sounds weird to refer to her over and over again as Senator Landrieu in our own home. What I meant to say was, 'Landrieu will talk about charter schools in general, and I will focus on the importance of education here in our community and the bank's support of the network.'"

That sounded better to me, and I eyed Frances to see if she liked my enhanced version. "Okay," she said, seeming satisfied. "I hope it all goes well."

As she was walking out the door for her job at St. Dominic School in Lakeview, she glanced back at me over her shoulder and said, "Say hello to '*Mary*' for me." I stifled a smile, musing that her sarcasm was perhaps a punishment for calling the senator by her first name as if we were good friends.

More than once, I had thought that wives, including Frances, sometimes functioned as governors of their husbands' self-esteem by whittling down their egos a bit when necessary. They wanted it never too high and never too low—in other words, restrained and tolerable. Perhaps she felt mine was surging a bit too high for my own good this morning and decided to knock me down a peg.

Hours later, my excitement fizzled into disappointment. The press conference had been canceled due to the approaching storm, and I was crossing the Medard Nelson parking lot to return to my car. I noticed that morning how hot and sweaty I felt, and my excitement was gone. The $250,000 check was still in my pocket, untouched, its edges curling slightly in the heat. Disappointment slowly turned into annoyance.

"Pfft—Tropical Storm Katrina," I muttered as I unlocked my car. I had already evacuated for two other storms that summer of 2005, but both had turned out to be false alarms, and both were poorly executed. The thought of subjecting my family to another contraflow evacuation greatly irritated me. *Katrina isn't even a hurricane anymore after weakening from crossing Florida*, I thought in frustration.

I wondered if meteorologists thought that the tropical storm would re-enter the gulf and strengthen again. Who knew? I just knew that this morning the community wouldn't get to hear about the children at Medard—mostly disadvantaged students—who would now get much better resources in their pursuit for a good education. There would be no television interviews, no newspaper write-ups, and no check presentation. There would be nothing this morning. I can't even remember if I said anything to Senator Landrieu before everyone scattered.

Before getting in my car, I looked back and checked out the newly renovated school. It was beautiful, a great improvement over the previous facility. The administrators, the community, the parents—everyone had worked so hard. I admired the structure one last time before starting the engine.

The new charter school was evidence of the collaborative efforts of those who believed a good education system was vital to maintaining a vibrant business community. Proud New Orleanians were clearly starting to reverse the declining trends in economic development, education, and political leadership, areas that all needed to be better if we wanted to attract new companies to our region.

New Orleans had even elected a former Cox Cable executive as mayor, Clarence Ray Nagin, who was not a career politician. Nagin ran on a platform of "economic development, job creation, and keeping our young people home," another sign that New Orleans voters yearned to revitalize the city's commerce.

And, in a letter he sent to the business community in 2004, Nagin said, "I look forward to working with you to make New Orleans a cradle of opportunity for our children." Things, to me, looked brighter than ever.

However, I had no idea that the Medard Nelson building, St. Dominic in Lakeview, our exciting education reform initiatives, our hopes for improved economic development opportunities, and roughly 80 percent of New Orleans itself would be under water and almost completely destroyed in just a few days.

TWO DAYS
BEFORE THE STORM

Saturday, August 27, 2005

10:00 a.m.

Discouraged by the canceled press conference, and dismissing the approaching storm as hype, I looked for a nice distraction to cheer me up that weekend. The city's two beloved sports teams certainly did the trick. The Saints and the Hornets were about to embark on what we hoped would be historic seasons.

The Saints' first exhibition of the NFL season kicked off at the Superdome against the Ravens, and we were firmly confident that the contest would be the first step toward the first Super Bowl championship in the team's 38-year history. The Hornets, meanwhile, were about two months away from tipping off their fourth NBA season since moving to New Orleans from Charlotte. Many took the fact that New Orleans could now support two pro sports teams to mean that our city's corporate fortunes were as encouraging as they had been in eons.

And that wasn't all that was on my mind. The opening day of dove season—usually the first Saturday in September—was right around the corner. I had talked with one of my fellow hunting buddies, Ross Wales, about getting a better class of firearm. So I decided that checking out the new shotguns that had arrived at a local sporting goods store in Metairie would be the perfect way to spend a Saturday.

Ross and I had worked at Hibernia together for nearly twenty years. The sale of Hibernia was scheduled for the first week of September, and the two of us were expecting a nice payday from the stock options we had earned over the years. We agreed to upgrade our hunting guns as soon as the bank transaction was finalized, but not a day sooner. It would be a small present to ourselves, a memento of our hard work that we could enjoy together for many years as colleagues and hunting buddies.

I called my friend, and he agreed to accompany me to Puglia's, the sporting goods store in Metairie that doubled as a hangout for sportsmen in the area. Anything a hunter or fisherman could think to want was in that store, which crammed a full Bass Pro outlet's worth of items into a fraction of the space. It was a place that wives abhorred but that their outdoorsmen husbands loved.

After surveying the place's vast inventory, I picked out a twelve-gauge Beretta shotgun I wanted and asked the salesman to put it away for me for a couple of days. Ross and I had agreed that neither of us would buy a gun until after the bank sale. Our decision to wait was not because of the money—we just did not want to jinx the bank deal. I told the salesman I'd take it but that I didn't want to buy it until the next week.

The salesman frowned and said, "Sir, I'm sorry, but I can't do that. This is our busiest time of the year with dove season upon us, and the demand for our shotguns is very high. Look, this is the prettiest one in the case. If you want it, I would encourage you to buy it today. I'm sorry, but the store won't allow me to put it away. It won't last long," he warned.

I looked at Ross to see what he thought. "The bank sale is going to happen in a couple of days, right?" I asked. "So, what's the big deal, huh?"

The salesman studied us, clutching the gun stock as if he were ready to put it back in the display case if we took too long. It offended me to imagine some unworthy hunter swooping in between now and next week to buy my shotgun.

"Yeah, it's gonna happen," Ross said. He added, "What could happen in a couple of days? You're not going to jinx it."

I was still a little anxious about violating our earlier rule of waiting, but I took one more look at the gun, and I was sold. "Okay, I'll take it now," I said. "Ring it up."

After the clerk had rung up my purchase, he slid my shotgun into a custom case, handed it over, and we strutted out of the building.

On the way home, I stopped by the bank and quickly carried out a few office tasks that were expected before a possible hurricane strike. But I wasn't convinced this puny storm could turn into a real threat. My mind was on better things, like the new shotgun waiting for me in my car.

Back at home, I walked in carrying the case and proudly set it down on the bench next to our piano. I couldn't wait to show my new bird gun to Chris, my middle child who shared my passion for hunting.

"What's that?" Frances asked.

I said, "That's the Beretta I've been talking about."

"I thought you were going to wait until after the bank was sold," Frances replied.

"Well, I couldn't wait," I said. "The man at the store said if I waited, somebody else was going to buy it because dove season is coming up and this is the busy season—and, well, I had to have it."

Frances stared me in the eye and chided, "That's the

oldest trick in the book. You should have waited. I hope you didn't jinx the deal."

I didn't exactly jinx the deal that day, but Frances' words still echo in my mind. As it would turn out, the bank deal would ultimately go through. But today, when I reflect on what would happen to our family and our city in the next few days, I can't help but wonder whether I jinxed something much more significant than the bank sale.

Frances just shook her head. She couldn't have known that, within a few days, the Beretta would be in her determined grip as she would survey the worst catastrophe of our lives.

She turned back to what she had been doing before I arrived and contemplated two bags and a small pile of clothes that were in front of her. I realized she was packing lightly for herself, Chris, and Katherine. She wasn't packing anything for me.

"Have you changed your mind about going?" Frances asked me. Her plan was to take a short trip to her mother's house in Pineville, in the central part of Louisiana. "The storm is strengthening, I hear."

On the television in the background, the news channels were in complete hurricane coverage mode. Every channel devoted its programming to the storm that wouldn't die. Just a day earlier, forecasters had predicted the Category 1 storm would weaken as it crossed Florida and meander north. But it had moved back into the warm waters of the Gulf of Mexico and strengthened again into a hurricane.

I thought about Frances' question. I had suffered through several evacuations in New Orleans, and some had turned out to be false alarms. Enough was enough. Frances could go north to her mother's if she wanted, but I was staying put. This storm may have ruined my big day on Friday, but I wouldn't let it ruin the whole weekend.

I shook my head. "I haven't changed my mind," I said,

firmly. "I may need to be here for the bank." The part about being here for the bank was a fib that she probably didn't buy, because she kept encouraging me to go.

"I'm not sure if the contraflow lanes are working any better, but the traffic should be lighter later tonight," she said. Her plan was to leave late in the evening.

"Pfft—'contraflow,'" I repeated sarcastically. The word alone made me nauseated. Contraflow was supposed to be a method of improving the flow of cars during an emergency in which both inbound and outbound interstate lanes become one-way roads leading out of the threatened area. But I'd suffered through failed attempts.

To me, 'contraflow' was code for a massive governmental screw-up, designed by some bureaucrat to torture its citizens. In frustration, my mind raced with sarcastic one-liners.

Contraflow. The tenth level of hell that was left out of Dante's Inferno.

If you really wanted to punish Sisyphus, you should've subjected him to an eternity of contraflow evacuations, not rolling a rock up and down a hill for all of time.

I attempted a joke with Frances. "Contraflow could be a true deterrent to crime. Like, a judge say could say, 'Sir, you are hereby sentenced to twenty years of contraflow for your horrible and heinous crimes.'" I imagined a hardened criminal buckling at the knees upon hearing the verdict.

Frances was undeterred and unamused. "Look, I'm packing for Chris, Katherine, and the dogs, and we are leaving in the Suburban," she said. "Why don't you come with us?"

"You're taking the dogs?" I protested. "Leave the dogs with me. They will be fine with me."

Frances countered, "If anything bad happens, you won't be able to take care of them. They're coming with us."

Somehow, Frances had managed to make "contraflow"

sound even more unappealing. Two adults, two kids, and our two golden retrievers, packed into a Suburban, crawling along the road for hours in contraflow. It really *was* the tenth level of hell.

I was hoping that the storm would turn, or lessen in strength, or go back where it came from—anything that would lessen the threat to New Orleans and also prevent us from having to endure another contraflow evacuation.

Instinctively, Frances knew we wouldn't be that lucky.

A Disastrous Experiment

I had experienced my fair share of bad evacuations.

My first experience with a large evacuation was when Hurricane Andrew threatened New Orleans in 1992. Hurricane Andrew would prove to be more difficult than just trying to get out of the city. Whatever chaos was happening outside was no match for the chaos *inside* our car. During the evacuation one of our sons, Chris, developed a fever so high that he began to go into convulsions. We were on Interstate 49, approximately ten miles north of Opelousas, Louisiana, when this occurred. We were in the middle of nowhere.

It's a helpless feeling to have a sick child without access to medical treatment. We were enormously blessed by a passing ambulance driver who saved Chris' life on his way to evacuating hospital patients from south Louisiana. I contend that I may hold the unofficial world record for the most "Hail Marys" and "Our Fathers" prayed while standing on the shoulder of an interstate highway.

The terrible experiences with evacuations didn't stop there. In 1998, Hurricane Georges prompted an even larger evacuation. The Superdome was opened as a shelter of last resort for those unable or unwilling to evacuate. Highways were hopelessly clogged, which caused the Louisiana Department of Transportation and Development as well as the Louisiana State Police to finally devise a better evacuation plan. The two hurricanes caused state officials to begin to reevaluate the emergency evacuation plans.

Their solution was contraflow. City officials were confident that reversing incoming traffic lanes during an emergency would improve the flow of cars in the outbound lanes.

They weren't the only people who had their minds on the importance of an evacuation plan. In 2001, the *Houston Chronicle* published a story predicting that a severe hurricane striking New Orleans "would strand 250,000 people or more, and probably kill one of 10 left behind. Thousands of refugees could land in Houston."

In September of 2004, the threat of Hurricane Ivan demanded that New Orleans officials put their theory to the test. The storm was threatening New Orleans, and Mayor Ray Nagin issued a call for voluntary evacuation at 6 p.m. on September 13th. Contraflow was implemented on a large scale for the first time. An estimated 600,000 or more in New Orleans and in surrounding areas heeded the call, all cars pointing outbound.

The concept was relatively simple, but it was difficult to execute. In fact, the first contraflow was a disastrous experience for everyone involved. The coordination wasn't smooth, resulting in significant delays. In best scenarios, it took at least triple the time to travel anywhere throughout the state. In other instances, it took more—the normal ninety-minute drive to Baton Rouge took up to eight hours for some evacuees.

One particular tragedy involved a friend's younger brother, who traveled in the 2004 contraflow for up to eight hours. Near the end of the trip he pulled over, complaining of a headache. He later died of an aneurism, likely due to sitting in his car for such an extended period of time.

His death illustrated the fact that the decision to

evacuate for a storm is usually not as clear cut as some—especially the media—make it out to be. The health and safety of family members must be taken into consideration. A lot of bad things can happen to a family in a car in heavy traffic, especially if there is no ready access to health care. This first contraflow during Hurricane Ivan would prove to be a valuable experience for an even greater storm, Katrina, the following summer.

My personal experiences of being stuck in a car with my ill son and learning about the—perhaps preventable—loss of my friend's brother caused me to be especially thoughtful before making a decision to evacuate for storms. I had become adamant that I would not subject myself to the misery of another failed contraflow unless absolutely necessary.

But in spite of these failures, I would soon learn that I had no choice but to try to join the contraflow again.

Saturday August 27, 2005
The Contraflow Surprise

11:30 p.m.

"Bill, Bill, wake up," I groggily heard Frances saying. She was gently shaking my shoulder. A little unsteady and not yet fully awake, I rubbed my eyes and squinted at the clock next to my bed. It was eleven thirty at night. The television was on one of the news channels, still streaming news coverage of the hurricane.

Before I was fully awake, she said, "We will be leaving in fifteen minutes, and I'm checking to see if you've changed your mind about going. The storm has really strengthened. You may want to take a look at this," she said, pointing to the television screen.

I sat up in bed sleepily and waited while my eyes focused on the screen. I couldn't believe what I was seeing. I focused my eyes and leaned forward to get a better look. "Oh my God," I said, stunned.

I had lived on the Gulf Coast for forty-five years, and I could not recall a storm as massive as the one that was taking over my television screen. The satellite image of the giant circular cloud looked like it covered the entire Gulf of Mexico. I simply couldn't believe the storm that was puny a couple of days before could have turned into such a massive, monstrous hurricane so quickly.

"Well, what do you think?" Frances asked, studying my face and my newly acquired respect for the storm.

"Frances, it's massive. The surge alone is going to cause major damage somewhere along the coast. The winds will also be bad, but the surge is really going to do some damage," I said, not taking my eyes off the satellite image.

Now that I was concerned, Frances was even more worried. "So, are you going with us?" she asked in a hopeful voice.

"Absolutely," I immediately replied. "And we are taking both your Suburban and the Expedition."

I jumped in my Expedition with only one change of clothes and my new Beretta. The opening day of dove season was upon us and I thought I might be able to sneak in a dove hunt or a skeet shoot over the weekend. I still had not yet fully grasped the seriousness of the situation. Frances and I both expected to return home in a couple of days after the storm passed.

Frances called her mother to let her know we were getting on the road and heading to her house. The trip would normally take just a little over three hours, but with contraflow traffic, we told her we had no idea when we would arrive.

We got onto westbound Interstate 10 from Causeway

Boulevard in Metairie, Frances in her Suburban and me following close behind in the Expedition. With both vehicles gassed up, we were fully prepared for the trip to take at least twice as long as the normal three hours. If we got separated, we both agreed to meet at a familiar service station about an hour away.

But we didn't get separated. And to our surprise, the traffic was moving remarkably well, even though the highway was full of other contraflowers. A little more than an hour later, we both pulled over at our predetermined destination to stretch our legs and walk the dogs. When I went inside to buy a water and some chips, I noticed the serious and somber looks on everyone's faces.

It appeared that everyone else was thinking the same thing that I was. This wasn't a false alarm to laugh at or to get mad about. This was the real deal, and everyone knew it. Instinctively, it seemed like people were resolved to act courteously so that everyone could contraflow the hell out of Dodge.

We got back in the vehicles and headed north to my mother-in-law's home in Pineville, Louisiana. Before I knew it, we were pulling into her driveway, where the diminutive, soft-spoken woman stood to welcome us. I looked over at the dashboard clock. It was three fifteen in the morning. I was shocked that we had arrived so fast.

Governor Kathleen Blanco's traffic plan had really worked this time. *Blanco must have finally worked the kinks out of the Contraflow design,* I thought to myself.

New Orleans had finally managed to execute a successful contraflow. It was indeed a surprise—but it would be the last pleasant surprise for some time. Within hours, we would be shocked by the fate of our city and of the New Orleanians back home who either could not or would not heed the call to evacuate.

Sunday, August 28, 2005
A Vicious Curveball

8:00 a.m.

When we woke up early Sunday morning after our trip, Frances' mom had prepared breakfast for us. The weather channel was on and the warnings from the newscasters had taken on a more ominous tone than the night before. The storm had become even more massive and consumed the entire Gulf of Mexico. The winds were measured at speeds that prompted newscasters to begin discussing the "worst case scenario."

As newscasters explained, the worst situation for New Orleans would be for a massive storm with a huge surge to travel right up the throat of the Mississippi River. And that's exactly where the storm appeared to be headed.

Anticipating a hurricane is a nerve-wracking experience. You know you're going to take a pounding, but you don't know whether to look for it from the left, the right, or up the middle. You do know, however, that it is on its way and that there is nothing left to do but cover up as much as possible and take the punishment—a hurricane rope-a-dope.

We had continued to watch television all of Sunday and into Sunday night, hanging on every word of every forecaster on at least six different channels, switching back and forth to see if any of them were offering any encouragement. Very little, if any, was to be found. The only sliver of good news was that the high winds had slowed just a bit to a Category 3 level.

However, I knew this would make little difference. The high winds had already created the surge and the water was going to get very high near the point of impact. The only hope for New Orleans was a last-minute shift east or west and that the water didn't breach the protective levees.

I woke up to my alarm at five o'clock on Monday morning. I wanted to get an early start at a temporary bank office in Alexandria, my home town right across the Red River from Pineville. As I got dressed, I realized how exhausted I was from the weekend events and from a restless night of sleep.

As I finished putting on my shoes for work and grabbed my keys, my mother-in-law appeared at the door. For a woman who didn't complain about anything, she seemed unusually concerned. "I'm sorry, Bill. I'm so sorry for you and Frances and the kids. And for all of your friends and for all those poor people down there," she said. "I'm so sorry."

She had seen her share of misery and life's curveballs and knew a vicious one was hurling our way.

PART TWO

UNPRECEDENTED DAMAGE

CHAPTER 3

THE STORM[2]

Monday, August 29, 2005

6:00 a.m.
With my mother-in-law's words in my mind, I arrived at Hibernia Bank's branch office in downtown Alexandria, Louisiana, 200 miles north of New Orleans. Our local president, Wayne Denley, and the local commercial manager, Kermit Pharris, had secured an office for me. I found the office, closed the door, and immediately picked up the phone to dial into a prearranged conference call.

I was a member of Hibernia's Incident Management Team, or IMT, which was the group charged with planning for and implementing disaster recovery efforts for the bank. Most of the team had evacuated to the primary disaster recovery site in Shreveport, some 330 miles to the north of New Orleans and well out of the hurricane's path. Dial-in numbers and reporting times had been circulated among the IMT members. The plan was for each manager to report in on his line of business as the storm passed over the city.

---

[2] Much of the information in this chapter, including numerical data, was derived from an account of Hibernia's recovery from hurricanes Katrina and Rita that was written by Russell Hoadley, retired Hibernia chief public affairs officer.

One IMT member had stayed behind in New Orleans. Steve Hebert, a twenty-one-year bank veteran and member of the IMT, was head of Hibernia's property management division. The stocky local had a quiet and unassuming demeanor that belied his intense work ethic and determination. Hebert managed the Hibernia Center in addition to 355 offices and other buildings across Louisiana and Texas.

Like me, Steve had not been particularly concerned about Katrina when it crossed Florida on Thursday, four days before. He had even gone to the Saints pre-season football game the Friday night before the storm, and he was in the company of thousands of other fans who were blissfully unaware. But reality did creep in at the end of the evening. Steve wasn't able to stay for the entire game, as the storm reports he was receiving from the bank continued to worsen by late Friday. Originally, the storm wasn't expected to hit New Orleans at all. But by Friday evening, the outlook had changed, and forecasters warned that the hurricane could become a Category 5 monster headed directly to New Orleans.

Hebert and his team had reacted by undertaking more serious storm preparations, focusing their attention on the operations center at 1111 Tulane Avenue, about four blocks from the bank's main office in downtown New Orleans. It housed the bank's mainframe computer, telecommunications systems, and network operations, all of which were vital for the bank to run. The brown and tan and box-shaped ten-story building looked inconspicuous from the outside—maybe that was intentional because it housed the bank's central nervous system.

In previous storms, a large mobile generator driven to the Hibernia Center on a specialized vehicle provided any emergency electrical power that might be necessary. But the generator had to be on the street next to the building, leaving it vulnerable to flooding. The bank, therefore, had purchased other emergency power equipment that could be installed on the roof of the Hibernia Center, above potential floodwater.

The equipment had been tested prior to the storm, and Hebert was highly confident that it would operate as intended. He and a few other employees decided to spend the night at Hibernia in a temporary command center to make sure the emergency power equipment operated smoothly.

6:10 a.m.

The storm arrived at dawn, slamming ashore near Buras, Louisiana, sixty-three miles downriver from New Orleans. The wind howled. Rain poured down.

Soon, all hell was breaking loose in New Orleans, where our operations team was on location in the middle of the worst part of the storm. This was a time when they really earned their money. They were a dedicated and highly competent group of people that had a reputation for going above and beyond for the bank.

The conference line opened, and at thirty-minute intervals, the IMT members would call to report in on their lines of business. I could hear the wind in the background and the anxiety in the voices of our operations group. It was a surreal feeling to hear the updates on the phone while also watching the weather channel hurricane coverage on the television in an office across the hall from me. In my office, two hundred miles north, the weather was overcast, but there were no high winds or even rain.

10:00 a.m.

By mid-morning, most of the high winds had passed New Orleans and all systems were still working. The effects of the storm didn't seem much different than from previous hurricanes.

Hebert and another employee, Jim Spiers, discovered

"a few ground floor windows blown out and a few inches of water on the lobby floor, which were mopped up during the day." When they stepped outside to survey the damage, they were pleased to see that Katrina's initial effects had mostly spared the building. Hebert was especially thankful that the mainframe computer operated normally.

They dialed into our system-wide conference call and reported that it appeared the bank had again weathered a giant storm. Everyone on the call brightened at Hebert's words, and we all breathed a sigh of relief—including me, in my temporary office in Alexandria.

People were heard passing around praise and expressing thanks that our bank had survived yet another big one. I could sense the relief in their voices.

Another call would be set for the next morning, and we all signed off. But our relief was premature.

At approximately 3 p.m., Hebert walked over to what was then called the Fairmont hotel, where he had a room reserved to wait out the storm. He needed a shower and some sleep, but he discovered that the hotel had no electricity or water. Puzzled at the lack of utilities, he walked back over to the Hibernia main office a few blocks away. The streets were empty except for scattered broken glass, but they were still relatively dry, and the office seemed fine.

Hebert didn't know things were about to be anything but fine in New Orleans. With no utilities at the Fairmont, Hebert walked back to the Hibernia Center to check on the bank's equipment. Later that evening, exhausted, he found a quiet corner to take a much-needed nap.

He wasn't able to nap for very long.

11:15 p.m.

Hebert was abruptly awakened by Spiers, who told him something was wrong. He told him water was flowing into downtown New Orleans.

Hebert went to the top of the ten-story Hibernia Center to get a better look. What he saw down Rampart Street shocked him.

The street was inundated with water, and more came. The first floor of the Hibernia Center was flooding again after water had gotten in and been mopped up earlier in the day.

Without access to a working television, Hebert couldn't have known that the federal protective levees around the city had toppled. The media was reporting that the storm surge had knocked out many parts of the protective levee systems around the city. Built below sea level and protected only by its levee system, the city some describe as a bowl was rapidly filling with water. The water flowed unimpeded directly toward the nervous system for all bank operations at the Hibernia Center.

Tuesday, August 30, 2005
One Day after the Storm

6:00 a.m.

The following morning, we signed back on for our next call. The winds had passed and most of the heavy rain had stopped, and everyone on the management call thought we had prevailed without much damage.

But something had clearly changed.

The tone of the Incident Management Team's conference call was much gloomier than the first one. The group reported that the water was now rising in the street and entering the Hibernia Center building. The employees said the floodwater was threatening some of the equipment and they had to sign off because they needed to move the equipment to a higher location. They didn't yet understand why the water was rising.

"If we weren't flooded from the rain, where is the water coming from?" they asked. It was obvious that Hebert and the operations team were scrambling to deal with the rising floodwater. The call was short, and the anxiety was intense.

That was the last call the whole team held. The next scheduled one didn't happen.

Communications on the dial-in had ceased, and I no longer had a direct line into what was happening in downtown New Orleans. No longer in telephone contact with the other members, I was puzzled at what was happening to the brave ones responsible for the Hibernia Center.

In the coming hours and days, we could only imagine what exactly Hebert and his team experienced as the circumstances around them deteriorated so rapidly. I would later learn that the situation was much worse at the Hibernia Center and for our courageous employees than I could have ever imagined.

10:30 a.m.

Scattered across the country, bank employees now obsessively watched the early morning hurricane coverage in horror.

Donald Barry, the head of our item processing division, had evacuated to Houston and was tuned in to NBC News' Brian Williams. Barry later recalled, "Williams was doing a live feed, knee-deep in water at the corner of Canal and Baronne streets."

Barry looked hard at the television. He knew the corner well. It was just around the corner from the Hibernia Center. He said, "That was the moment I knew we were going to be in very, very serious trouble. I thought about the doomsday scenario for New Orleans—about how it is a bowl—and realized we were going to see it play out."

Still in Alexandria 200 miles north, around mid-morning I peeled myself from the news and went downstairs into the bank parking lot to check on the weather. I walked outside and could see the clouds accumulating above, moving fast and in a circular pattern across the horizon. Intermittent rain was dropping as the storm headed north.

I walked back inside the bank building and passed the ATM machine. There were hundreds of ATM receipts lying on the floor. I waited a minute and saw a man come up to the machine to attempt to withdraw money. A slip of paper appeared. He looked at it, and then let it drop to the floor with the others that had accumulated. I picked up the receipt, and it read, "Out of Service." I began to grow increasingly concerned about our central nervous system at the Hibernia Center in New Orleans.

I let the receipt flutter down to rest on the floor with the other slips. I walked away, lost in my thoughts and oblivious to the fact that I had just passed local commercial manager Kermit Pharris in a hallway.

"Is everything okay?" Kermit asked me. He must have seen the concerned look on my face.

"I hope so," I told him. But I really didn't know what was happening to our bank and our team back in New Orleans. The winds and rain had stopped, so I couldn't figure out what could be the problem.

I didn't have time to wonder what was happening to Hebert and team as they waged their battle at the Hibernia Center. The rest of the Hibernia managers and I were tasked with developing our own contingency plans. Even though none of us had the exact details from Hebert, by now everyone knew through the national media coverage that New Orleans had been badly damaged and that we would have to quickly convene to assess the impact on the bank, our employees, and our customers.

With New Orleans uninhabitable and electricity and phones out in Baton Rouge, the commercial head of the bank established a command center in Lafayette, Louisiana, approximately 200 miles west of New Orleans and an area that was mostly spared from the worst impact of Katrina. This would be convenient for me as my older sister lived just south of Lafayette in the small town of Abbeville.

Most of us arrived at the Lafayette Hibernia main office on Tuesday afternoon, and we immediately began the daunting task of evaluating the impact. Each manager was asked to locate their people and then to report any special needs or missing employees. Fortunately, the bank prepared well for emergencies, and most of this work was completed later Tuesday evening.

A separate team was working on the systems and our physical facilities, so the next biggest job was to understand the impact on our customers. This effort was considerably more difficult. It required us to begin working from early in the morning until very late in the evening.

Meanwhile, back in New Orleans, Hebert's primary worry was the welfare of the employees and their families who had chosen to loyally stay at the Hibernia Center. While he had water and food, he wasn't sure how long that supply would last. He also worried about the municipal water supply to the building and the critical computer systems.

As our former chief public affairs officer Russell Hoadley later put it, "There was a simple reason why city water was so critical: It was used by the large air conditioning system in the building, which itself was essential to the operation of the heat generating computers. Without water, the AC would fail. Without AC, the computers would fail. Without computers, banking services would fail."

If that devastating domino effect occurred, the bank technology team would need to create special backup tapes of the banks' customer data to avoid a servicing catastrophe. Once the backup tapes were created, the team would have to transport that precious data to the backup mainframe system in Dallas.

His mind racing with thoughts of all that could go wrong, Hebert set about devising an improvised contingency plan for Louisiana's largest bank, whose headquarters were in a city filling up with floodwater rushing over toppled levees. Hebert reached out to his boss, Walter Walker. Walker pointed out that there were now only three ways to evacuate people and the critical bank tapes: "by boat, by helicopter, or by amphibious vehicle."

Wednesday, August 31, 2005
Two Days after the Storm

8:00 a.m.

The conditions in New Orleans continued to worsen. Food and water ran low. The critical mainframe computers at the Hibernia Center were still in danger. The diesel fuel powering the emergency generators at the building was limited, and the flooded city streets ruled out any chance of going somewhere to refuel the diesel tanks.

As if that wasn't enough, Hebert fretted about the looting and civil disorder he witnessed around the Hibernia Center. Vandals had already broken building windows and had attempted to break open an ATM. A Walgreens pharmacy across the street had been robbed.

Hebert had power for perhaps another couple of days, but that was about it. It was getting to be too much, and Hebert made up his mind that it was time to evacuate. After considering his options, he decided on helicopters as their way out.

Hebert went to work on an improvised rescue plan with Ben Gautreaux, Hibernia's technology risk manager. Gautreaux had joined the bank through the acquisition of Argent Bank almost ten years earlier and had relocated to

Shreveport's command center before the storm. He was a thirty-year banker and a native of south Louisiana, an area that provided services to the offshore oil and gas industry. Gautreaux was familiar with the major energy service companies operating offshore, and many were clients of the bank.

Gautreaux reached out to Brian Cheramie, an industry veteran, an old friend of his and a customer of mine. Brian's family was in the offshore supply boat business, bringing supplies and men and women out to offshore rigs. Cheramie was also an officer of SEACOR, a company that operated boats as well as helicopters through its subsidiary, Era. Cheramie quickly connected Gautreaux with Jerry Umfeet of Era. "Jerry put his fleet on hold for us," Gautreaux recalled. "He had oil rigs to service, but he was willing to help Hibernia out."

Together, Gautreaux and Hebert considered a plan for the people that were at Hibernia Center—at least 34 men, women, and children, not to mention two dogs. They had to take into account the problem of where to land the helicopters. The roof of the Hibernia Center was not strong enough to bear the weight of a helicopter loaded with people.

Hebert began scouring the skyline for other suitable buildings when he saw helicopters evacuating patients at the Tulane University Medical Center about two blocks away. He felt sure that was the place to turn to, but he wasn't certain how to get the people and the tapes from the Hibernia Center through the floodwater to get there. Gautreaux went back to Cheramie to see if they could also provide life rafts. Cheramie assured them they could.

The plan was for the helicopters to drop three rafts onto the Hibernia Center roof. Hebert and others would inflate the rafts downstairs and the families and employees—toting the computer tapes—would climb aboard. Some of the men volunteered to wade through the water to pull the rafts along.

But now Hebert needed to get permission to land the helicopters on the roof of the hospital. He found some Louisiana Wildlife and Fisheries agents who were helping supervise the air evacuation at the hospital. Unfortunately, the floodwaters did not wash away the red tape. The agents informed Hebert he would have to get approval from City Hall first.

The amazing Hebert was undeterred. He trudged down to City Hall through the water and met an official there. Hebert would later remember that his biggest fear in walking through the dark water was falling through a manhole into the sewer below. When he finally arrived, that official gave Hebert the permission he needed. The plan was ready. The helicopters were given the green light to rescue the Hibernia employees and their families.

However, one more obstacle remained. There was a miscommunication on the first attempt to land the helicopters. As a result, the helicopters had to turn back to Houma and wait for the following day because nighttime had arrived.

Crestfallen, Hebert and the other families had to spend another night in a deserted building, hoping to be rescued when the following day broke. That night, with little food and water and no bedding, the Hibernia group slept restlessly on a lower floor of the building.

They could hear gunshots in the distance.

Thursday, September 1, 2005
Three Days after the Storm

7:30 a.m.

The next morning, Hebert connected with Cindy Haygood, a Hibernia employee and a member of the National Guard. With Haygood's help, Gautreaux secured an authorization code for the helicopters to return through the restricted airspace to rescue the stranded families and bank tapes.

The helicopters finally arrived. The families loaded themselves into the helicopters and successfully left the area. After the evacuees joined other bank employees and friends in Houma, the tapes were loaded onto a chartered jet and whisked off to the backup mainframe computer in Dallas.

Hebert, Gautreaux, Cheramie, and other bank employees had avoided a major customer service catastrophe. The loss of the tapes combined with the physical effects of the hurricanes would have devastated our customers financially and perhaps even the bank itself.

Thanks to these people and their bold creativity, our customers had the information and tools with which to begin getting through the aftermath of the storm. The bank could begin the true work of recovery.

Now, with the worst of the crisis over at the bank, I assessed the needs of my wife and kids, who were staying with my sister in Abbeville. It was clear that the New Orleans offices would be shut down for the foreseeable future, and the most logical place for my family to relocate would be Houston. But our immediate problem was that we didn't have any clothing or essential belongings for an extended stay in a distant city. We had left town with little more than the clothes on our backs, expecting to return quickly.

As I drove from my makeshift office in Lafayette to my sister's home in Abbeville that evening, I formed a plan. I would make a quick drive back to New Orleans the next morning to grab some necessary belongings, and I would return to the bank in Lafayette later in the day to complete assessments. I pulled into my sister's driveway in Abbeville, satisfied with my plan.

A "John Wayne Dude"

As difficult as our days were, Hebert's decisive plan to rescue employees from Hibernia—and my own quick plan to gather my family's belongings—was a stark contrast to the plans that were being made for the people back home. Tens of thousands of people, mostly African American, were stranded in New Orleans and still suffering.

They were gathered at the Superdome, which had earlier been designated as a shelter of last resort. Large numbers had also gathered at the Ernest N. Morial Convention Center, though it was neither a shelter nor a designated evacuation point. People had simply assumed, incorrectly, that such a large public building would be a safe place to stay. Still others were trapped on elevated sections of Interstate 10, sandwiched between flooded sections of highway below them.

The primary plan Governor Blanco and Mayor Ray Nagin had for the city seemed to involve only the pre-hurricane landfall contraflow. That plan was—by most accounts, including mine—well executed, at least for those who had the opportunity to evacuate. However, the post-landfall response overwhelmed state and local officials, and the city descended into chaos. The high floodwaters cut off access to the city. Water and food supplies diminished, and public facilities could neither operate nor be accessed by citizens.

Each night, worldwide television audiences viewed images that became increasingly desperate by the hour. There were widespread reports of lootings and vandalism. New Orleanians watched in horror as rescue attempts remained delayed. Watching from the living room at my sister's house, I'll never forget the image of the little boy, no more than three or four years old, whose lower lip quivered while he was trapped at the convention center and being held by his mother.

Then, President George W. Bush appointed Lieutenant

General Russel L. Honoré as commander of the Joint Task Force Katrina. And things improved decisively.

Honoré is a self-described African American Creole from Point Coupee Parish in central Louisiana. His gruff, no-nonsense style contrasted sharply with local politicians, and the results were almost immediate. Even Mayor Nagin agreed in a radio interview on Thursday night, September 1st, "Now, I will tell you this—and I give the president some credit on this—he sent one *John Wayne* dude down here who can get some stuff done, and his name is General Honoré. And he came off the doggone chopper, and he started cussing and people started moving. And he's getting some stuff done."[3]

On Friday, September 2, Honoré was filmed shouting orders to his armed troops near the convention center, including one unforgettable directive to "put those damned weapons down" and that they were on a humanitarian relief mission, not a combat mission.

Honoré remained on the scene until well after the Superdome and convention center had been evacuated by September 4th, which was just two days after he took charge in New Orleans. His efforts during New Orleans' darkest hour would later earn him the Omar N. Bradley "Spirit of Independence" award.

After hearing about the arrival of Honoré late Thursday night—and with a good understanding of New Orleans' geography—I was encouraged that I might be able to enter the city. I figured I would access the city through Airline Highway, quickly find some needed items, and then quickly return to Abbeville.

I figured wrong.

---

[3] Information derived from "The John Wayne dude who's kicking butts and getting stuff done," The Guardian, September 8, 2005: http://www.theguardian.com/world/2005/sep/08/hurricanekatrina.usa2.

NEW ORLEANS, LA. (Oct. 10, 2005) - President George W. Bush greets Commander, Joint Task Force Katrina, U.S. Army Lt. Gen. Russel Honoré, and Director of FEMA Relief Efforts, U.S. Coast Guard Vice Adm. Thad W. Allen as he steps off Air Force One on board Naval Air Station Joint Reserve Base, New Orleans. President Bush and the first lady meet with top ranking military officials at NAS JRB, New Orleans to receive briefs on Joint Task Force Katrina relief efforts. The Navy's involvement in humanitarian assistance operations are led by the Federal Emergency Management Agency (FEMA), in conjunction with the Department of Defense. U.S. Navy photo by Photographer's Mate 2nd Class William Townsend (RELEASED). Courtesy of Wikimedia Commons.

METARIE, LA. (Aug. 31, 2005): I-10 at Causeway Boulevard. In the great floods of most of Greater New Orleans in the aftermath of Hurricane Katrina, this was the area of the last bit of unflooded passable highway out of town, and hence was one of the main evacuation stations for Hurricane Katrina victims. Courtesy of Wikimedia Commons.

Bill Herrington, Mary Landrieu, and Leslie Jacobs discussing charter schools at the University of New Orleans. Photo courtesy of James Meza, 2004.

NEW ORLEANS, LA. (Aug. 29, 2005) - Aerial of a flooded neighborhood. New Orleans is being evacuated as a result of floods from hurricane Katrina. Thousand of people have been rescued from the flood waters by moving to their roofs and attics. Air view over I-10 by intersection of City Park Avenue/Metairie Road, with section of Greenwood Cemetery visible at left, portion of Metairie Cemetery at right. Photo by Jocelyn Augustino/FEMA Courtesy of Wikimedia Commons.

CITY OF NEW ORLEANS
C. RAY NAGIN, MAYOR

March 19, 2004

Mr. Bill Herrington
Hibernia National Bank
P. O. Box 61540
New Orleans, LA 70161

Dear Mr. Herrington,

When I ran for Mayor three years ago, economic development, job creation and keeping our young people at home were some of my major goals. With the reorganization of New Orleans Regional Chamber of Commerce and Metrovision into Greater New Orleans Inc, we have the tools and vision to create new opportunities for our citizens.

I know that the year-long effort to reorganize and implement the change has not been easy. Despite the difficulties of the shift, you have succeeded. Without your leadership, this vision would not be possible. On behalf of the City of New Orleans, I offer my sincere appreciation for your efforts toward the realization of our mutual goals. I look forward to working with you to make New Orleans a cradle of opportunity for our children.

Sincerely,

C. Ray Nagin
Mayor

CHAPTER 4

HEARTBREAK AT AIRLINE HIGHWAY AND CAUSEWAY

Friday, September 2, 2005
Four Days after the Storm

2:00 a.m.

Early the next morning, I slipped out of bed and into my jeans, quietly so as to not disturb Frances. I turned off my alarm before it could wake me. Truth be told, I really didn't need it—I hadn't slept a wink. My mind had been racing all night from one worry to another.

After a few minutes, I gently cracked the door. I nearly escaped, but Frances' head popped up. The bedside lamp came on.

"You're not leaving me,'" she said, her eyes squinting in the lamplight and her eyebrows furrowed.

Frances had told me the evening before that she was going to New Orleans with me to gather our clothing and other personal effects. But I had no intention of letting her join the excursion. I wanted her to stay in Abbeville, where I thought she was safer.

"Yes, Frances. I am going by myself," I replied with a hushed but firm tone.

I had explained to her last night—and I explained again

now—why she should not accompany me to New Orleans: It was unsafe, and she may slow me down.

Officials had widely disseminated warnings to not attempt to enter New Orleans. Reports of lootings, murders, flooding, and downed power lines had dominated the local and national news, though many of those reports were later found to be exaggerated or baseless. The National Guard and General Honoré had been called in to restore order and protect the poor souls who had not escaped Katrina. The authorities had locked down the city—a forbidden zone of entry, except for the military.

None of the news reports had indicated problems in my area, Old Metairie. All of the media reports had focused on the isolated flooding in Lakeview, the downtown area including the Superdome, and the Ninth Ward. But I didn't want to take any chances. I would find a way to quickly get in, grab some basic necessities, and get out.

But while I spoke, Frances calmly got dressed in a pair of overalls (that I didn't know she had), slipped on her tennis shoes, and pulled on my favorite purple Hornets cap.

"Okay, I'm ready. Let's go," she said.

"You're not going," I told her as she walked past me and into the kitchen. It's difficult to raise your voice toward your wife at two in the morning when you are a guest in someone else's home.

My sister Dianne was aware of my scheme to leave without Frances, and she was in the kitchen with a pot of coffee already prepared. I poured my coffee and pulled Dianne aside.

"Look, you need to help me explain to her that she needs to stay here. She is just going to slow me down and get emotional and get in the way," I told Dianne. I paused for a moment to look for Frances and realized that she had disappeared from the kitchen. "Where did she go?" I asked.

"She went outside," Dianne said. "I think I see her sitting in your Expedition."

"Dammit," I muttered, annoyed. I marched out to the car, opened the driver door and bluntly told her she couldn't go. By this time, she had found the Beretta shotgun I bought from Puglia's before the storm and was gripping the barrel with her left hand. The butt of the gun was on the floor board, the end of the barrel pointing up. She was leaning forward in the passenger seat looking straight ahead, the Hornets cap low to her brow.

"Get in and let's go," she said. "You're wasting time."

I shook my head and whispered "dammit" for the second time that morning, something I had done many times before when defeated in our marital squabbles. It was 2:15 a.m. by then. We waved goodbye to my sister and her husband, Jimmy, and headed out for New Orleans.

Hatching an Unlikely Plan

Neither of us talked much for the first twenty minutes of the ride to New Orleans. Frances had barely moved from her original position: slightly forward and alert on the edge of the passenger seat, the twelve-gauge still firmly in her hand and her gaze fixed straight ahead. If not for the tension of the moment, I would have busted out laughing at the sight of five-foot, two-inch Frances, armed and ready for battle, right down to her personalized Hornets helmet. Her curly brown "morning hair" was pooching out from the sides of the cap. It's a vision I will never forget.

As we headed down U.S. 90 on the two-and-a-half-hour journey, I was thinking about my conversation with Frances the night before.

"How will you even get into the city?" she had asked

in a defiant tone. "They are not letting anyone in. Do you have a plan?"

Feigning confidence, I had explained, "They are not letting anyone in to New Orleans, but we live in *Old Metairie*, which has no flooding and no looting. There is nothing to worry about."

She didn't buy it. Her voice on edge, she said, "Then why are you bringing your shotgun, and why don't you want me to go?"

"Well, there might be *a little* to worry about," I calmly explained.

"Like what?" she stubbornly continued.

I said, "Well, I don't know exactly. I just want to be prepared."

"You have no idea what you're doing, and you don't have a plan," she chided.

"I have a plan and don't you worry about it," I said, defensively. However, she was right. I had nothing.

Right then, for the first time, we spotted a law enforcement presence several miles ahead. There were several patrol cars on each side of the road with red lights flashing. A line of about twenty cars were inching along, and I could see that the officers were directing the drivers to turn around and abandon any hope of venturing into St. Charles Parish, just west of Jefferson Parish and Metairie, my ultimate destination.

The silence in the Expedition was finally broken when Frances, still looking straight ahead, said, "They are not letting anyone in, and we are going to have to turn around."

"No," I said. "This is the St. Charles parish line, and I have a *plan* to get in." That was about 10 percent honest, as I bounced around a semi-plan in my head.

"Well, what's the plan?" she asked, finally turned and looking directly at me while still gripping the shotgun barrel.

"Well," I said, "first thing, slide that shotgun into the floorboard of the back seat."

Fortunately, she complied with my request. It was the first time that morning that had happened. About ten cars were now ahead of us. One by one, all of those in front of us were being directed to turn around.

Frances said, "Okay, now what?"

I replied, "Find everything with Hibernia on it that you can. Hats, name tags, papers, whatever." Having worked at Hibernia for nearly twenty years, my Expedition was well stocked with various bank merchandise and trinkets.

I immediately found my name tag and put it on my shirt. Frances dug out a green baseball hat with Hibernia emblazoned on it. It was crumpled and dirty and not at all befitting the head of a corporate banker, but it had to do for now. Now the fifth car in line, I scrambled for every Hibernia item within reach in order to make me appear as officially part of the bank as possible. Frances dug for more stuff while muttering about the lack of a plan when she miraculously discovered one final piece of Hibernia treasure: a zippered green money pouch that I used as a youth baseball coach to hold concession stand money.

"Perfect!" I exclaimed and placed it strategically on the dashboard, where the deputy would easily spot it with his flashlight.

We were now just two cars back, and my mind raced as "the plan" came together. I hadn't yet made a believer out of Frances, though. She was thoroughly confused, agitated, and worried, and I could tell because she was looking at me with palpable skepticism.

"Calm down, look straight ahead, and let me do all of the talking," I told her. Surprisingly, for the second time that trip, she complied.

With just one car ahead of us, I turned on my inside light, looked into the rear view mirror and made myself look as official as possible. I straightened my name tag. I adjusted my crumpled cap. I eased the Expedition forward.

When we arrived to him, an awaiting sheriff's deputy said, "Sir, this is the St. Charles Parish line, and no one is allowed to proceed beyond this point." He added, with an authoritative tone, "You are going to have to turn around." With his flashlight, he scanned the interior of the Expedition and the profile of Frances, who sat stoically next to me.

I waited for his light to reflect off of my official-looking Hibernia name tag and then responded, "Officer, my name is Bill Herrington, and I work for Hibernia National Bank." I emphasized the word "National" as if it would somehow elevate my status to the officer. "My client is the Jefferson Parish Sheriff's Office and Chief Deputy Newell Normand, and I can't get in touch with them. It's been almost a week since I've heard anything, and I don't know if they are getting paid!"

Before quieting down, I asked the deputy, "Are they getting paid?"

I didn't mention Normand's name by accident. At the time, he was second-in-command of the Sheriff's Office. And my invoking Normand's name visibly perplexed the deputy, who called his partner over to discuss.

"Hey, Joe," he said in a voice loud enough for us to hear. "This guy is with the bank, and he's trying to get the deputies paid in Jefferson Parish. I don't know if those guys are getting paid."

Joe shrugged his shoulders and offered no assistance to his fellow deputy. Joe's fellow deputy paused for a bit and then leaned in to get a better look at me and my stone-faced passenger. "Look," he said. "I don't know if those guys are getting paid. I'm gonna let you through, but they will likely make you turn around when you hit the Jefferson Parish line."

I nodded my head and said, "Okay." I thanked the deputy for his good judgment.

Buoyed by my successful act of persuasion, I moved forward with Frances confidently. I glanced back in my rearview mirror to see the next car in line being directed to turn around.

About thirty seconds passed before Frances broke the silence in the car. "And that was your plan?" she asked.

Sitting tall in the seat and obviously pleased with my own performance, I replied, "Well, it worked, didn't it?"

She shot back, "But you weren't honest with the deputy."

I disagreed. I said, "I wasn't *dishonest* with him. The Sheriff's Office *is* our client, and I'm trying to make sure *everyone* is getting paid, including the deputies. Plus, have you forgotten that I have to report to the bank in Houston on Monday in order to make sure people are actually getting paid, and we don't have any clothes at all? This is sort of an emergency, don't you think?"

I was feeling a bit guilty about stretching the story with the deputy. But I made a mental note to myself to confess to Chief Deputy Normand when I next saw him. Hopefully, he would understand the extraordinary circumstances we were in.

We continued our journey down U.S. 90 toward New Orleans. Frances continued looking straight ahead, sensing that I now had a renewed sense of purpose and realizing I had a slight grin on my face. The trip had taken on a new dimension for me. It had become a quest to prove to my wife—to myself—that I had the street smarts to navigate through the blockades when others could not.

My ego was battling my brain. And the ego was winning.

The Eeriest Sight

As the St. Charles deputy had warned me, there was another checkpoint at the Jefferson Parish line. It was around four thirty in the morning when flashing lights appeared ahead again. The line of cars was longer than the St. Charles line, but the result was the same. Not a single vehicle ahead of us was allowed to pass, and each one had to turn around.

But our confidence was bolstered by our first encounter, and Frances and I assembled even more Hibernia booty for display. I eased up to the Jefferson deputy and again explained who I was. I emphasized the words "Chief Deputy Newell Normand" in my plea.

The deputy obviously knew Normand ranked only under Jefferson Parish Sheriff Harry Lee. He understood the implication of my message and did not bother to consult with the other deputies. I'm not sure if he was more focused on the prospect of not getting paid or that I confidently communicated Chief Deputy Normand was my client. Whatever the case, the combined message of money and power was too strong for him to ignore.

Before waving us through, he explained that few, if any, cars were ahead of us. There were reports of downed power lines and debris on the highway. Safe passage to New Orleans was doubtful at best. He told us to be careful, and he wished us luck. It wasn't so much what he said, but the tone of his message made it very clear to us that we were in a very uncertain situation.

For the first time, I had serious doubts about the wisdom of my plan, and I even considered turning around. But we kept going.

I traveled a bit slower now, following the officer's warning about highway obstructions. The last thing I needed was to damage our car on an abandoned highway. And make no mistake about it—it was totally abandoned. There were no other cars on either side of the split highway. It was pitch-black dark, with no lights visible at all except for those on our Expedition.

We approached the Hale Boggs Bridge which crosses the Mississippi River. When we got to the top of the bridge, there was only one light visible on the horizon. Off to our left, a flame burned at the Shell refinery in the town of Norco. We were elevated above our surroundings and looked all around. There were no lights as far as we could see except for that sole refinery flare. The only other sensation was a strong smell of sulfur.

We didn't belong here.

Our anxiety grew. I gripped the steering wheel with both hands and leaned forward, alert to anything that might obstruct our path. "*This adventure was a very bad idea,*" I thought to myself.

The first exit off the bridge after crossing the river was Airline Highway. Driving very slowly, I took the exit and carefully merged onto Airline. With my high beams on, the damage predicted by the deputy became more apparent. Trash and debris blew onto the highway, and we swerved and dodged numerous hazards. Our eyes were wide open, hoping to catch any threats before it was too late.

Although I knew I was on Airline Highway, I couldn't tell exactly where I was. The first landmark appeared on the left side of the highway. Slightly foggy and still very dark, the outline of a tall structure appeared. Trying to get my bearings, I asked Frances if she could make it out. We slowed down to study the structure.

We were shocked to realize it was the air traffic tower at the Louis Armstrong International Airport in Kenner. It was one of the eeriest sights I've ever witnessed. The tower and the surrounding runways were completely dark. There wasn't a single light on—not even a runway light.

We continued down Airline and discussed our plan to enter our home. We would quickly run up to our house and spend no more than fifteen minutes collecting the essentials for us and our three children. The plan was for me to watch the front door for looters and for Frances to quickly grab and bag clothing, valuables, and a few other items to tide us over until we could return to secure the rest of our effects.

When she was done, I would look for that check for the charter school. I had come home with the $250,000 check because of the evacuation. It was in the house somewhere, and I needed to find it.

Our plan was set: In and out. Fifteen minutes. Then back on the road to Abbeville.

We forged on. We were surprised when we saw the first evidence of human activity. Down the highway off to the right, we could see light. As we approached, even more slowly now, it almost appeared like a high school football stadium lit up for a Friday night game.

We soon realized the military had established a sort of camp on the parking lot of Zephyr Field, the home of the New Orleans' AAA minor league baseball team. From a distance, it reminded me of a cable news network's coverage of an overseas war. There were helicopters, tents, and trucks. Various military vehicles had completely taken over the stadium parking lot.

It was now around five o'clock in the morning, and I could see a couple of men dressed in military fatigues walking around the makeshift camp. I felt sure that this was the end of the line of our trip, and I prepared myself to be stopped by the military authorities. I told Frances to continue to look straight ahead, and I would do my best to talk my way through if we were stopped.

With the sky now illuminated by the lights of the military, I sped up and approached the base camp. One of the guys looked up, eyeing our vehicle. He studied us for a bit, and I felt sure he would direct us to pull over. But he turned away, apparently satisfied that we were no threat.

As we passed the parking lot, a Black Hawk helicopter

prepared to lift off as men piled in. I couldn't believe what we were witnessing. Most first responders for hurricanes are typically the Red Cross or a church group. But that wasn't the case for this kind of devastation. Our first responder was the military. I didn't know it then, but soon, I would be up close and personal with yet another Black Hawk.

Having made it safely past the military camp, Frances and I again went over our plan to enter our home, now just a few miles away. Dawn was approaching, and we could see more of the city. Roofs, buildings, and signs were strewn all about. We passed the Saints' practice facility and then the Southern Eagle Budweiser building, which had a sign and part of its roof both down. This seemed strange because the grounds there always struck me with how well maintained they were. Both the Saints and Southern Eagle were clients, and I had good friends there. I wondered how they were going to function in a city without citizens.

I knew that the Causeway Boulevard underpass was likely flooded, so I took the access ramp over the top. Although dawn was peeking, I could still barely see. I proceeded slowly around a traffic circle and toward the exit ramp, progressing slowly down the decline.

I slammed on my brakes.

The sudden stop startled Frances. She squealed in a high pitch. I couldn't believe what I saw before me.

From where I was positioned on the ramp above Airline, I could see water standing at the base of the incline. The water lapped at the base of the ramp. It had become a boat launch, not a main highway exit. I looked over to my left and saw what appeared to be a bread truck in a parking lot. The water was over the hood.

Our home was just a few blocks away. We both stared in disbelief and realized—for the first time—that our home had probably flooded badly. It felt like we'd discovered a crime scene.

Now stopped on the down ramp with my headlights shining into the floodwater, I realized that I was in danger of being rear ended by any other surprised drivers that might be behind me. I knew I had to back out of there.

I put the Ford into reverse and slowly navigated backward toward the Causeway circle and onto the highest elevation above the highway below. As we slowly backed away from the horror, I prayed no one would come around and plow into the rear of our car. Thankfully, we made it back to the Causeway circle, a couple of stories above the flooded highway below.

Now able to see more of the skyline, we were still the only car visible on the horizon. With the morning light slowly but steadily breaking through, we had an unobstructed view down Airline Highway and toward the center of the city of New Orleans. Airline Highway and surrounding shopping centers, businesses, Metairie Country Club, and neighborhoods were flooded for miles—flooding as far as the eye could see.

Frances and I were stunned silent. It was then that I realized our lives, and those of so many others, were now completely changed.

Up until that moment, we had assumed through the media coverage that the flooding of the city was only in specific areas and not broadly across the whole of New Orleans. We knew the damage was bad—very bad—but that it was isolated and relatively easy to fix, we thought. But now we could see, with our own eyes, the enormity of the destruction. No amount of policy changes, education reform, or economic development was going to be enough to address this disaster for a very long time. In fact, all of the previous hard work and progress that the area had made was in total jeopardy. I was in shock. I had no idea what to do.

Our hearts broke simultaneously, right there, parked on Causeway Boulevard above Airline Highway.

Flooding the "Saucer"

As it turns out, floodwaters had plagued New Orleans since it was first established back in 1718. It hadn't taken long for the new French settlers to discover the perils of being situated there.

In addition to being subjected to annual seasonal flooding from the Mississippi River from April to August, hurricanes swept through the area from June to October. Founder Jean Baptiste Le Moyne, Sieur de Bienville, reported that the river filled the new settlement with "half a foot of water" in April 1719. Then, in 1722, a hurricane destroyed most of the new French colonial city.

There was no denying that New Orleans had been founded in a very unfortunate location. By 1723, the original settlement was laid out as fourteen city blocks, with drainage ditches around each block. In the years after the 1719 flood, officials built a series of levees and drainage canals, and the city battled back against the floodwaters as best it could.

Nonetheless, as explained in a paper written in 2012 by Tulane Professor Stephen A. Nelson, there were five reasons why New Orleans would remain vulnerable to flooding from hurricanes as time marched on. Like the Houston-Galveston area, its proximity to the Gulf of Mexico and rising sea levels were problems. And its elevation was not only low—it was below sea level. To make matters worse, New Orleans faced two additional problems: erosion and its gradual but persistent state of sinking, which is caused by compaction of sediments deposited by the Mississippi River over thousands of years.

Therefore, as it matured over the years, the city bolstered its preparedness by developing a protection system containing levees to keep water out of New Orleans' residential areas as well as manmade outfall canals and screw pumps to help drain water out when necessary. Throughout the years, higher elevation ridges had formed along the banks of the Mississippi and Lake Pontchartrain, and man-made floodwalls connected them to create a "system" of elevated rings around the city—a system of lips, if you will.

But the areas inside the "lips" nonetheless remained much lower. This included large portions of swampland that had been drained to build homes in the city's neighborhoods such as Lakeview, with many of those sections that had been developed after 1900 now well below sea level. Many have observed that the New Orleans area's layout resembled a "bowl." I prefer the term saucer, because the depths of the lowest part of the area are indiscernible to an untrained eye.

Despite all of that, I chose to move to New Orleans in 1986 and raise my family in the saucer partly because government officials assured residents that the system protecting them from the elements would stand up to a storm the size of Katrina.

But Katrina ultimately revealed that the metal planks that were supposed to reinforce the New Orleans protective system's levees and floodwalls didn't run deep enough. The soil below the levees and floodwalls proved to be much less stable than authorities realized, and they gave way during Katrina, killing at least 1,429 people and causing more than $200 billion of damage.

It became clear too late that officials had underestimated the problem of the area's subsiding soil. Combined with the weak drainage system and the increased vulnerability to hurricanes, it was a problem that had been brewing for generations—and now it had been unleashed on New Orleans with shocking ferocity.

As a task force evaluating the performance of New Orleans' hurricane protection during Katrina wrote in its final report, "The System did not perform as a system.

The hurricane protection in New Orleans and Southeast Louisiana was a system in name only. The system's performance was compromised by the incompleteness of the system, the inconsistency in levels of protection, and the lack of redundancy. Incomplete sections of the system resulted in sections with lower protective elevations or transitions between types and levels of protection that were weak spots."

Now, standing out on Causeway Boulevard, Frances and I joined the hundreds of thousands who were left to begin picking up the pieces.

METAIRIE, LA. (Aug. 30, 2005) - Celebration Church and Airline Village shopping complex on Airline Highway in floodwaters. Neighborhoods throughout Greater New Orleans are flooded as a result of Hurricane Katrina. The Herrington home is in the top right of this photo Courtesy of Wikimedia Commons.

METAIRIE, LA. (Aug. 30, 2005) - Neighborhoods throughout Greater New Orleans are flooded as a result of Hurricane Katrina and the failure of the Federal levee system. In some areas fires have started due to electrical outages. Jocelyn Augustino/FEMA. Metairie Country Club is shown in this photo. Courtesy of Wikimedia Commons.

Old Jefferson suburb of New Orleans, LA, September 7, 2005 -- Base of operations for the FEMA Urban Search and Rescue response teams is shown from the air. Jocelyn Augustino/FEMA. Helicopters shown landed at Zephyr Field on Airline Highway. Photo courtesy of Wikimedia Commons.

NEW ORLEANS, LA. (Sept. 9, 2005) - Jesuit School at Banks and Carrollton, with trees down. Still a good bit of standing water, reflecting part of the scene, though flood waters have been drained a few feet down by this time. Photo by Infrogmation. Courtesy of Wikimedia Commons.

CHAPTER 5

FIFTEEN MINUTES
AND FOUR HEFTY BAGS

Friday, September 2, 2005
Four Days after the Storm

7:00 a.m.

As we drove slowly north up the Causeway toward Metairie Road, Frances and I prepared ourselves for the reality that our neighborhood would most certainly be flooded and we discussed various options for how to get to our home. Our plan was to drive down Metairie Road and wind our way through side streets to get as close to our home as possible. From there, we would wade to our house.

We realized we had progressed as far as we could when we reached the edge of the floodwater. We stopped the car, turned off the engine, and stared at the scene before us. After a few silent moments, we got out of the car.

The normally bustling Old Metairie neighborhood was eerily hushed: no cars, no people, and no chirping birds. There was nothing that helped define our neighborhood. It was void of any sign of life.

Frances and I stood together on the curb, at the brink of the floodwater in our neighborhood. We looked hopelessly toward the direction of our home a few blocks away. Clutching my Beretta shotgun, I tried to gather my wits to comprehend what I was seeing, feeling, and sensing. Silently, we moved down the street.

After a block or two, we heard a faint sound. It was mechanical. We realized it was the sound of a generator and walked toward it. The sound got louder and louder as we approached.

Then, unexpectedly, we saw the outline of a person walking in a yard. Holding my shotgun over my shoulder, I walked slowly toward the figure. Now just a hundred or so yards away, the shadow stopped and stared in our direction. We also stopped. We studied the person and contemplated our next move. Was it a looter? A homeless person? A trapped neighbor?

Something told me this person was not a threat. I laid the shotgun on the ground and told Frances to stay put while I approached the stranger. We each slowly walked toward each other until we were twenty or so yards apart, which was close enough to eye each other but far enough to keep a safe distance.

We quickly identified ourselves and moved even closer together. His name was E.J. Raley. I waved for Frances to join me and greet our new acquaintance when someone else appeared. E.J. introduced him as his good friend Jay Cuccia, who was a resident in the high and dry area of Old Metairie and the owner of the small generator that we had heard.

Our new friend E.J. turned out to be a local Allstate insurance agent who was looking for someone to help. He and Jay had made their way to the city and had hauled their flatboat to Old Metairie in search of someone in need of assistance. However, they had not found anyone there to be helped—until we showed up. We explained our predicament, and E.J. quickly offered a solution.

They offered to drive us up Labarre Road to the edge of the water and launch their boat to take us to our home.

We immediately accepted. We hopped in his truck and prepared ourselves for the boat ride home.

This wasn't the dramatic rescue he had hoped for—no hacking through a roof with an axe as we had seen on television. A mini-rescue in the form of only a short boat ride would have to do. Little did E.J. know that the bigger rescue was just on the horizon.

Black Stew

E.J. pushed off of the railroad levee at Labarre, and now Jay slowly directed the fifteen-foot flat-bottomed boat down Edinburgh toward our home. I was very familiar with both the boat and its Go-Devil motor as I had been hunting and fishing in south Louisiana since I was a child. It was designed for two people, maybe three in emergencies. Four people was pushing it. But I wasn't about to leave Frances behind. And off we went headed for our flooded home on Bath Street.

The area had been around since 1839, when surveyor E.A. Springbett prepared plans for the Town of Bath No. 1 and Bath No. 2 in Metairie. A resort hotel was built at Bath No. 1, near Lake Ponchartrain, where visitors came to swim, fish, and dine. The resort was named after the town of Bath in southwest England, 12 miles east-southeast of Bristol.

Bath No. 2 was located at Airline highway, and the two were connected by a railroad right-of-way, which today is Bonnabel Boulevard. The long-forgotten town of Bath survives today in the form of a short odd-sounding street in Metarie: our street. The street originally was a continuation of Bonnabel, between Airline Highway and the Southern Railway tracks. I had built my family's home on Bath Street.

As we motored along, the extent of the devastation became very clear to Frances and me. We passed downed power lines and mangled, naked trees that had been stripped of limbs and leaves. Branches protruded through the water's surface. The damaged trees were the most visible evidence of the mighty power of the storm that had unleashed its fury on the area. Dodging the downed trees and navigating through the murky water reminded me more of a boat ride to one of my favorite south Louisiana wood duck holes than a ride through my old familiar neighborhood.

Overcast but with dawn fully arrived, we chugged quietly through the stagnant water that had mixed with the hot air; it had turned into a black, stinking stew. It produced an awful smell I'd never forget. Even today, I can pick up a book from our attic that still carries the faint but unmistakable stench of that stew, an unwelcome memory of the day.

We passed abandoned cars that were flooded over their tops. Roofs were torn away from homes, exposing attics and living spaces. As we continued down Edinburgh, we cringed at the sight of the Starlights' home and yard, which was completely flooded. Our middle child, Chris, had played at the Starlight home countless times.

"Take a left up there, Jay," I said, almost whispering. "That is our street up ahead. Bath Street."

It didn't seem to be the familiar neighborhood we knew and loved. My thoughts drifted to years earlier, when we had first built our two-story home among the mostly older one-story homes in Old Metairie. I had been looking for a safe place to raise my family that would be near a playground. I loved sports as a kid, and I wanted my children to be able to ride their bikes to a safe athletic complex. I knew finding such a place in an urban area was not easy, so I had asked my friend, Chief Deputy Newell Normand, if he knew of an area where crime was low and that was near a playground where I wouldn't worry as much about my children's safety.

Newell had immediately recommended the Beverly Knoll subdivision. It was an area of modest older homes tucked away on the edge of Old Metairie that were being torn down for newer and bigger ones. And it was an area of almost zero crime, within a few blocks of what was then known as Metairie Playground, described to me as the best playground in the city.

Sold! And over the eight years we lived there, it proved to be a nice, safe place to raise our family. The kids had worn a path between our home and Metairie Playground.

"Bill and Frances," Jay broke into my thoughts. "I know you guys are probably in shock right now. You expected to pull right up to your house and get in and get out. We are both really sorry and can't imagine what you are feeling right now."

He paused again to make sure we were listening. We were.

"But it's real important that you hear me for a minute," he continued. "You are going to be very sad when you see your house. We understand. We've been through this kind of thing before. But we really aren't supposed to be here, and it's still very dangerous. We need you to think about what you really need and get in and out as soon as possible. Do you think you can do that for me?" He was looking us both right in the eyes.

"Yes, we can do that," I said, turning to Frances. "Right babe? We can do that, huh?" Frances nodded but didn't speak. She had claimed her spot in the boat next to me, asserting that she could swim well. She couldn't.

"Okay, good," said Jay. "We brought a roll of black contractor bags for you to put your things in. It's not the regular kind of hefty bag, but a real heavy bag designed to carry a lot. So, put everything you need to in there. The bags are not going to break unless it's really overloaded."

We nodded. I directed Jay to our home on Bath Street, not

knowing exactly what we would see but knowing it would be bad. As we rode along in the boat, I thought about a conversation I'd had with a good friend and mentor of mine.

He had been through a very difficult period in business, and I had admired the way he stayed rock solid during his crisis. Years later, when I asked him how he had coped, he told me that he sometimes visited the cancer ward at Houston's Children's Hospital. No matter what difficulties he had experienced during the week, he said the sick children in the hospital allowed him to realize how lucky he was, that his difficult time would pass. I reflected on his words for strength.

I continued talking to reassure Frances, reminding her that we didn't lose family, as so many others had. I told her that everything was replaceable through hard work and insurance.

What I didn't tell her was that I was very uncertain if we had flood insurance at all.

The Essentials

I began developing a mental list of only what we needed and could transport on the boat. "Okay, here's what we're gonna do," I told Frances as we continued toward our street. "You take the upstairs, and I will take the downstairs. Go into each of the four bedrooms upstairs and fill a separate bag with enough clothing for all of us for a couple of weeks. We'll be able to come back later once the water is pumped out of the city and get whatever else we want."

"Okay," she agreed, biting her bottom lip but still holding it together.

"But take nothing else that we don't need, babe," I said. "This is really important. This is a small boat and we can't load it with stuff we don't absolutely need."

She nodded her head again, this time a tear rolling down her cheek.

I pressed on, hoping to keep her mind on the mission. "Then I'm going to take the downstairs. Let's talk through what we need downstairs. So, what do you need down there?" I asked, hoping to keep her focused.

Surprisingly, she was doing pretty well. "Okay. Well, I'm worried about my mother's silverware. It's in the dining room in my silver box in the corner. I don't want the looters to get that. Will you get that for me?"

"Okay," I agreed. "I'll get that."

"And your uncle's painting. The one of the Austin hill country bluebonnets. I'm worried about mold getting on his painting, and I want you to get that."

"But that's not essential—," I began.

She cut me off. "It's been hanging in our home since we were married, and I want it. We're going to need it," she implored.

"Okay, I'll get that too."

She continued, "I can't think clearly now and don't know what will fit, but look around and get anything else we need."

Okay, that was good, I thought. *She's thinking somewhat clearly. We might be able to pull this off without a disaster.*

"And I want one thing that belongs to each of the kids. We won't be coming home for a long time, and they're going to need something that reminds them of home," she said, her voice cracking.

"Okay," I said. I sensed that she was in danger of falling apart now.

"I want to get Katherine's phone. The pink one I got for her room. She loves that phone."

"Okay, you can get that. That's a good idea," I encouraged her.

"And for Chris, I want his baseball glove," she said as

the boat slowly continued, our home now ten houses down on the left. "And William . . . poor William. He's away at college and doesn't know what's happening. I want to get his Hornets jersey."

Now our home was just five houses away. "Will you get that for William?" she asked me.

"Yes, I'll get that too," I said, my arm around her as I pulled her closer to me and reached out for her hand. We were only three houses away now. Clutching her hand and pulling her close to my chest, I said, "No matter what you see, you have to be tough. Okay? Really tough. We need to get in and get out."

"Okay," I barely heard her say, "I'll be tough."

We passed an old oak tree, and there it was.

I never fully understood the phrase "it takes your breath away" until that instant.

It is a gut-wrenching emotional experience to witness the mass destruction of your home and neighborhood. I was holding it together well. I was more in shock than sad. But I wasn't breathing.

I couldn't breathe.

I was trying to comfort Frances with my words, but the words wouldn't come out. I cleared my throat once, and then again, and then again. It was as if I'd been punched in the solar plexus.

The boat was now in our front yard, slowly approaching our front porch. I had built the house three feet off the ground, but water still had filled the house.

Jay advised me that I would need to get out and tie the rope around the front column. I wasn't even sure I could get the door open. I jumped out and put the key in the door and pushed, but the warm water had swelled the door and it wouldn't open. I pressed again, put my shoulder against it, and forced opened the door.

The Piano

A house full of water is strangely unfamiliar and nearly unrecognizable. I glanced up the hallway and into the dining room. Floating pillows, papers, and Coke bottles were the first things I saw.

I stepped back outside and reminded Frances to be strong. She reassured me that she would be. I turned around and asked her to jump on my back. After she did, I eased back inside the house and waded down the hall toward the family room, my eyes quickly surveying the rooms as we walked. I was taking small steps as the muddy water had made the wood floors—now buckled—very slippery.

As we entered the family room, the toughest sight to see was that of our piano, which three generations had played. My mother, sister, brother, and I had all learned to play on that instrument.

In our home, my oldest son William began picking out tunes on the piano when he was a toddler. He would become a skilled piano player, accompanying Frances and Timmy Todd "Mr. Timmy" during Mass. In a story published in the local newspaper on June 10, 1999, *The Times-Picayune* profiled William with a photo of him sitting at his keyboard in St. Dominic Church on Harrison Avenue. Later, Ronald Markham, Irvin Mayfield's manager and my buddy from the business group Greater New Orleans, Inc. (GNO) had taught William to play "stride" piano on it, a jazz piano style which emphasizes the rhythmic action of the left hand. William would go on to attend the New Orleans Center for Creative Arts and create a number of compositions on this piano.

No more stride. No more compositions, I thought as I watched the water lap against the sides in little waves. The piano bench was completely underwater. Our son's work, the tunes he kept inside the instrument's bench, were now gone forever.

I slogged toward the staircase and let Frances off on the landing. As previously planned, she quickly scaled the stairs into the upstairs bedrooms. With Frances off my back, I turned back around. My job was to find a few things to bag and take back before the mold got to them.

But I just bumbled around in the water, still amazed at what I was seeing. Old Metairie was supposed to be higher than other areas. And I had built the house another three feet from the base elevation. Yet here I was, looking at over two feet of water in the house.

I walked toward the kitchen and surveyed the bar stools where my kids used to sit while eating breakfast before school. There was now just a small pool of water in the seats of the bar stools, where the water had peaked. I looked in the seat of the first bar stool, where Frances always put my papers so I would remember to take them to work. A wet envelope was all that was in the seat of the stool. I picked it up and recognized that it was the $250,000 cashier's check I was supposed to present at the New Beginnings Medard Nelson charter school just a week earlier.

I walked to the kitchen, dodging various belongings floating in the water: Tupperware containers, a lunch box for one of the kids, and a solitary wooden spoon. The electricity had been off for nearly a week, and I knew I would have to open the refrigerator sooner or later. I opted for sooner and cracked the fridge and freezer doors. A bag of okra Frances had put up for a future gumbo fell out and floated in the water. The stench from what remained was overwhelming.

I moved toward the rear of the house and lifted the blinds to look outside. It was a sea of water, the pool completely submerged and unrecognizable. *This is going to be one hell of a mess to clean up,* I thought.

After stumbling around for a few minutes, Frances called down to ask how I was doing with my job. Stunned, I really hadn't made much progress at all. I shook myself out of it and then started to find what I could. With very little left downstairs to save, I first tried to find her silver in the dining room. I had to step slowly around the room, using my feet to find it as I couldn't see through the muddy water. I finally found what was left of the silver box and began putting the silverware into the bag. I then headed toward my uncle's painting. It was hanging in the entry way and the invading mold had not yet reached it.

It was interesting to see what possessions I decided to rescue given fifteen minutes and four plastic bags. It also occurred to me that I didn't care much about most of the stuff we had accumulated over the years that had been destroyed. I suppose it's because that's what most of it was just *stuff*. It could be replaced over time.

The few things I decided to bag or that made me sad to lose had some kind of special memory attached. One of these was a bottle of Buffalo Trace bourbon from the distillery of Bill Goldring, one of the bank's most important customers. Frances would later ask why I had bothered to save a bottle of booze. It was the #100 bottle in the first production run I would explain. And this was a reminder of a big deal I had completed. I found a few other items, including our photo albums and wedding pictures, and took them outside.

As I passed a bag to E.J. to put in the boat, he quietly said, "Bill, it's time to wrap up."

I went back upstairs to check on Frances. She had done a great job of finding essentials for all of us for the next couple of weeks. She had my suits and a few ties and a separate bag for each of the kids. Each had one treasured possession each of the kids would want that would later remind them of the home they once had: the pink phone for

Kat, some Hornets stuff for William, and Chris' baseball glove. I brought each of the bags downstairs and loaded them in the boat. I then went back to the staircase landing to put Frances on my back.

"Did you get the painting?" she asked. I told her I had.

"How about my momma's silver box?" I told her I'd gotten that too, not bothering to explain that the box had fallen apart as I tried to pick it up. We trudged our way down the hall and to the front door and slowly turned around one last time.

"I'll fix it for you, Frances. It's hard to see now, but one day it will be as good as new," I said, doing my best to remain positive but not really believing the words I just said.

We took one last look and then I lifted Frances up and back in the boat. I untied the rope and hopped in, and E.J. started the Go-Devil motor. We began our journey back to the launch.

Looking back at our house as we left, I could see the roof of William's car in the driveway. The top of the car was just inches above the water. The yard was full of debris. My neighbor's big tree had fallen over and destroyed my wood fence, wedging itself between several of my pine trees. *Another big job to fix,* I thought to myself.

E.J. explained that he needed to check the house of another friend, and we said okay. So we motored down the flooded street, loaded with four people, four big bags of possessions, a painting, and a bottle of booze. We made our way to the house down Edinburgh Street, which was also in the direction of Metairie Playground, and observed the damage.

We traveled a bit farther down Edinburgh, closer to what had been my family's beloved playground. By then, the spot was named Pontiff Playground, after the local baseball phenom Wally Pontiff, who starred at LSU and won the College World Series before his sudden death in

2002 from an undetected heart defect. And I realized Pontiff Playground was not spared by the floodwater, which had destroyed all of the buildings, baseball fields, playground equipment and everything else there, all the reasons why I had moved there in the first place.

Through the fence I could see that Metairie Country Club was also completely flooded, extending over to the multi-million dollar houses on the perimeter of the country club. That's near where tycoons and captains of industry lived, as well as many other successful entrepreneurs in the city. It was yet another reminder that the flood had affected every economic sector in New Orleans.

E.J. surveyed his friend's house and the situation, shaking his head in disbelief at the scale of the destruction and then slowly turning the boat around. "I'd like to go back the back way along the railroad levee if we can make it," he said. "We might as well check to see if there is anyone else back here before we leave."

Hoping that we would not find a poor soul left in this carnage, now almost a week old, we all agreed, saying, "Yes, let's do that."

Reaching the levee road, we headed back toward our earlier launch spot. We went down a couple hundred yards when we encountered a downed tree blocking the street. In order to continue on, we would have to maneuver the boat around the tree up into the yard of another house. Slowly moving the boat around the tree, and periodically bumping into unidentified submerged things, we got within fifteen feet of a house near the corner of Jefferson and Loumor Avenues.

Traveling slowly with the engine purring, E.J., still at the front of the boat, held up his hand. "Did you hear that?" he asked, his ear cocked. "I heard something. Turn off the motor."

We turned off the motor and listened. The air was thick

with silence. None of the rest of us heard anything. *How could he have heard anything over the sound of the boat motor?* I thought to myself.

But E.J. *had* heard something—and he was about to embark on the big rescue he'd hoped for.

CHAPTER 6

THE RESCUE

Friday, September 2, 2005
Four Days after the Storm

11:30 a.m.

"Help!"

This time we all heard the muffled cry for help, not just E.J. But we couldn't tell exactly where it was coming from. We looked around but didn't see anyone. Finally realizing that the source of the sound was a small house on the corner, we paddled closer to the front window of the residence.

We still didn't see anyone, but we could definitely hear something.

The brick, one-story home we approached was older and small, probably built in the post-World War II housing boom. The address was 475 Jefferson Avenue. Many similar homes were being torn down in our neighborhood to make way for more modern two-story houses. It had a mailbox mounted on a pole in the front yard, and the name "Harrigan" was visible on the box, just above the surface of the floodwater.

With the motor now off, E.J. leaned over the front of the boat to better hear the voice in the home. "Hello?" he said, raising his voice a bit. The typical sounds of the neighborhood were gone. There were no cars and no people, just the foreign, faint sound of helicopters in the distance.

"Hello?" E.J. called again. "Is anyone in there?" He pulled the boat up to the house, just under the front window. "Hello?" E.J. said again.

This time, the voice of an older man responded. "I'm here. Go around to the back."

The window was open, but a screen on it was closed. The interior blinds were shut, and we couldn't see who or what was inside.

"Go around to the back," the voice pleaded again.

But there was no way back there. Downed trees blocked the way, and a carport canopy had collapsed, further preventing passage.

"Sir," E.J. said. "Your trees are down, and there is no way to get to the back. Can you pull up your blinds so that we can see you?"

The voice repeated, "Go around to the back."

Frances, Jay, E.J., and I all looked around at each other, puzzled at the instructions.

E.J. said, "Sir, we are here to help you. The only way out for you is through this window. If you can raise the blinds, we will come in and help you get out." A minute seemed to pass, but there was no response. Everyone on the boat continued to look at each other in confusion.

Then, the shades came up.

Guns and Crucifixes

An elderly man stood at the window with a rosary hanging around his neck, holding a .38 caliber revolver. E.J. recoiled. I had gotten up from my seat and stood just behind E.J., who was on his hands and knees, leaning forward at the front of the boat. We were all startled at the sight.

"Whoa, sir!" E.J. said. "We're here to help you, but you are going to have to give me that gun."

"You're not getting my gun," the man immediately responded.

We hesitated as we weighed the predicament we were in. Was the man deranged after spending almost a week in his flooded home alone? Did he think we were there to loot or harm him? E.J. and I looked at each other as we mulled the next move. I glanced back toward Frances and read the name on the mailbox past her shoulder.

"Mr. Harrigan," I said, slowly. "I'm Bill Herrington, and I'm your neighbor. We're not here to hurt you. We are here to help you. But we can't do anything until you give us that gun." I paused for a moment before adding, "Is the gun loaded?"

"Yes, it's loaded," he replied, holding the gun with a hand that appeared to have been strengthened by manual labor over the years. He wore a determined look on his face, and in a stronger voice he said he was willing to fire the gun if he had to.

E.J. and I paused again. E.J. said, "Mr. Harrigan, we are here to help you, but we can't do anything until you give us that gun."

Again, he said, "You're not getting my gun."

I stared at the contrast between the gun in his hand and the crucifix around his neck, an image that would always stay with me. Finally, after an uncomfortable pause, E.J. spoke up.

"If you won't give me your gun, let me unload it, and I will give the gun back to you. Would that be okay?" E.J. asked.

Mr. Harrigan remained visibly wary of the boat full of strangers hauling bags full of items with them. After some consideration, he said, "Okay." He then handed E.J. the gun through the window, and E.J. unloaded the revolver handing the bullets to me. I put the bullets into my pocket, and we said, "Okay, we're coming in."

E.J. and I climbed through the front window. Mr. Harrigan appeared to be in his early 80s, living alone in his home. He was dressed only in his underwear, his T-shirt, and the rosary dangling around his neck. I looked around his bedroom and noticed medicine and his glasses on the bedside table. There were about eight rosaries hanging from different spots in the room.

"Mr. Harrigan, we are going to get you out of here," I said. "Let's get some of your things together and put them in this bag so you can get to a better place."

By then, he seemed convinced our intentions were good, so he placed his unloaded gun on the bed. We quickly gathered his medicine, glasses, rosaries, and some clothes, and we put them in a bag. He slipped into some pants, and we helped him through the window.

After conferring about the best way to load an octogenarian into a fifteen-foot flatboat already carrying too much, we navigated the window and helped Mr. Harrigan settle in to a seat next to Frances in the middle of the boat. E.J. pushed off, and we were on our way again, with five people and five bags loaded in a boat built to support half its current load.

As we moved up Jefferson, Mr. Harrigan hunched over and fixed his eyes on the bottom of the boat. "I was in the war," he whispered, touching the crucifix around his neck. "Never thought I'd see devastation like that again."

I presumed he meant World War II because of his age, but I didn't have the nerve to ask. The old man had first survived a storm from hell and then a terrible flood before enduring nearly a week in isolation.

"I was at the end of my rope. I'd lost hope until I heard your motor," he said, still looking down. "If you hadn't come along, I was about to . . . " His voice trailed off, and nobody said a word.

Mr. Harrigan buried his face into his large hands and

wept. Frances dug out a shirt to wrap around Mr. Harrigan's shoulders. It was as sad a sight as I'd ever seen.

Left alone to my thoughts, I pondered how just fifteen minutes beforehand I had been feeling sorry for myself. But now, I realized how much worse off Mr. Harrigan had been. I was still stunned, but I didn't feel as gloomy as I had felt before the rescue.

As Frances' mother had wisely said many times to me before, "It could always be worse." I realized that Mr. Harrigan—old and alone—was going to have a much tougher time after this storm than my family and I would.

The Choppers

The sound of a helicopter overhead cut into my thoughts. Apparently patrolling the area, the pilot of a Black Hawk spotted our boat, and the chopper hovered about two hundred feet above us. An armed soldier looked down at us from out of an open side door. The sight was menacing.

Not feeling terribly lucky on this day, it occurred to me that the soldier may have been trying to determine if we were good guys or bad guys—whether to save or shoot us. I decided it would be wise to help him understand we were good guys, so I looked up and extended my hand above Mr. Harrigan's head, pointing down toward him. I hoped that would convey to the soldier that we were rescuing people, not looting them.

The Black Hawk continued to hover for a bit before it was suddenly joined by an orange Coast Guard chopper about fifty yards to its left. There we were, puttering along with Black Hawk and Coast Guard helicopters lingering above us. I don't know if they were discussing whether we would be friends or foes.

But soon the Black Hawk took off, and a man in an

orange jumpsuit appeared out the Coast Guard chopper's side door. He looked down at us and pointed to a spot on the tracks. I presumed he wanted us to take Mr. Harrigan there. I waved to him that I understood, and the helicopter moved a few hundred yards over to that position.

We continued up Jefferson past our neighbor's homes, including our good friends, the Casey's. We kept surveying the devastation. My neighbor, Mike Rodrigue, lived on the corner. He owns the Acme Oyster House chain of restaurants, the most notable of which is in the French Quarter on Iberville Street. Mike always had fancy cars and boats. His company's color is fire engine red, and his cars and boats were all that color. Mike must have evacuated like we did, expecting to return in a couple of days to resume his normal life.

His wife's red convertible was in the driveway, completely submerged in the dirty floodwater. His boat—one I had admired countless times—had floated off of the trailer and lodged itself between Mike's home and the neighbors'. I remember fearing that Mike might be devastated at losing his house, his boat, and his car.

We made it past Mike's house and arrived at the spot on the levee. Somehow, the Coast Guard rescue "swimmer" was already on the ground and waved us over to him. The helicopter had dropped him off and retreated for a distance. I could see that it had lowered a basket I assumed was intended to scoop up Mr. Harrigan.

As we reached the levee, I told Frances to begin taking our things out of the boat while E.J. and I helped load Mr. Harrigan into the basket. I stood next to the Coast Guard swimmer and explained to him that Mr. Harrigan was a war veteran and that perhaps he could be taken to a military hospital. The swimmer gestured that he understood.

The chopper approached us again as Frances unloaded the bags and painting from the boat. I could see the basket clearly and feel the wind from the chopper's blades as it came closer. The further down it came, the stronger the wind felt. Soon, we put Mr. Harrigan into the basket. The helicopter lifted the rescue swimmer up and again hovered overhead.

We All Have Problems

With Mr. Harrigan now safely in the basket, I looked over at our pile of belongings. Maddeningly, the wind had blown some of our possessions back in the water. I ran over to the bags and yelled for Frances to join me. We both jumped onto the bags to stop them from being blown off the boat. We ended up face down on four Hefty bags worth of possessions, gazing at each other on the railroad levee near the edge of the floodwater.

Somehow, Frances wore a slight smile as she looked at me. There was very little to smile about at that moment, so perhaps she realized I needed a boost. I looked over her shoulder and realized one of our wedding photos had been blown into the water, slowly sinking below the surface. The photo was yet another of our possessions lost to the watery grave Katrina had dug.

I looked away from Frances toward the helicopter in time to catch a glimpse of my uncle's painting—a large framed canvas of Austin Hill Country bluebonnets—getting blown end over end down the tracks. *Perfect*, I thought. *The one thing in the house Frances and I want is now tumbling down the tracks. God, if you are trying to send me a message, I've got it. You don't need to send any more.*

Atop our bags, I suddenly wondered if I had renewed the flood insurance on my home and belongings. I remembered arguing with my insurance agent that I didn't need flood insurance because I had built up so high. "If I get flooded, we all have problems," I remember saying. Now, my thinking was, *Well, you arrogant genius, we did get flooded, and we do ALL have problems.* A bad day got worse, and I found myself really hoping I had lost the argument with the agent.

I also worried about whether the helicopter had a camera on board, filming the rescue and us lying on our bags. I turned my head from the helicopter so my face wouldn't appear along with all of the other sad images we had been watching on CNN.

I still couldn't believe how quickly our fortunes had turned for the worse. Exactly one week before, I had been planning a presentation to the media in which I'd give a $250,000 check to a school alongside a U.S. Senator. Then, I felt victorious. Now, I was lying on four Hefty bags atop a railroad levee, watching helplessly as my wedding photos slipped into foul-smelling floodwater.

Days earlier, I expected to soon be loaded from the bank stock options that would become vested upon the sale of the bank. Now, I was likely not, due to the postponement of the merger. Life had changed in the blink of a hurricane's eye. Like my mother-in-law always said, things could always be worse. But at that moment, all I could think about was how things could also be a lot better. I had spent twenty years building up both my net worth and the life I had dreamed of, but at the time I feared it had all disappeared in the span of a few days.

Numerous thoughts swirled around in my brain. I now regretted talking my way into the city. Yet I also thought, *What would have happened to Mr. Harrigan if we had not come along at that time? He surely seemed like he couldn't stand the isolation much longer.*

Other thoughts overwhelmed me. *Why did I allow my wife to go with me? Why can't I remember if I even have flood insurance?* Then I realized Frances was still smiling at me. I was glad she was. She could just as easily have tried to drown me in the water for getting her into this mess, but she did not.

The helicopter soon flew away with Mr. Harrigan, and although I wasn't sure where it was going, I was glad he was safe inside the chopper. But I have no idea how E.J. was able to hear an old man's soft cry for help over the sound of a running boat motor. What I do know was that the man was nearly done, as he had told me in the boat, and I'm happy that we found him. If E.J. and Jay had not been there with their boat, I believe that one way or another there would have been at least one more casualty from the storm.

With the helicopter out of sight, Frances and I gathered our things and noticed that a stranded dog had found us. He limped along beside me. I have a soft spot for dogs, and the poor thing looked up at me and talked to me with his eyes. I couldn't be sure if this was true, but to me it was like he was asking me, *What the heck is going on? And when will it get better?* Perhaps he wondered why I didn't put him in the helicopter too. We threw the Hefty bags in the truck bed, and I gave the dog some biscuits and water I had in my Expedition before heading back to it.

When we arrived at the Expedition, I encountered Mike Rodrigue, who had also found his way to the neighborhood. He was standing at the edge of the water, in apparent shock, and staring helplessly toward the direction of his home. I had to give Mike the bad news that his home and his wife's car had been flooded.

Frances and I got back in the Expedition. Heading back to Abbeville, we both looked at each other, searching for something that would help us better understand what we had experienced that day. I wondered if this whole experience was some sort of nightmare.

As we drove back down the highway, I found Chief

Deputy Normand's phone number and dialed it. Unexpectedly, a woman immediately answered. I explained who I was and asked to speak to Chief Deputy Normand, not expecting that he would be available to pick up. The woman surprised me when she said she would put me through, and Normand picked up.

There was a lot of noise in the background, and it was clear that other sheriff's office employees were busily manning the phones, doing their best to manage the crisis. I quickly explained to Newell that we had found Mr. Harrigan and that he might want to send a boat back there to check for other stranded residents. He knew immediately where to look, which didn't surprise me, because he advised me about building a home in the area. I heard him shout a quick order to another deputy that we might still have people back there and to immediately check it out.

We hung up before I was able to confess to Newell how I had strategically mentioned his name to get past a deputy blockade and into the area. I would remember that omission in 2007, when Newell would go on to be elected to the office of sheriff in a landslide victory. And I remember it again today, as I write this story, hoping I don't get in trouble if he reads this.

I looked in the rearview mirror as our neighborhood became smaller in the distance. Frances and I were quiet, both thinking not only about our home but about our beloved church parish as well as our school, St. Dominic. Unlike the flooded surprise we discovered in Old Metairie, the news reports had been very clear that there was catastrophic flooding across that entire area surrounding our church and school.

Attempting to process the day's events, I turned my attention to the few belongings we were able to gather from the destruction. There were the bags and my uncle's painting, which we were able to retrieve from the tracks.

By some miracle, the painting itself was undamaged, save for a couple of chips on the frame.

Months later, that painting would be hung in a new Houston home, unrepaired, to remind myself daily that everything I own could be taken away in an instant.

CHAPTER 7

CONTRAFLOW TO HOUSTON

Saturday, September 3, 2005
Five Days after the Storm

By Saturday morning, the whole world knew the city of New Orleans would be shut down for the foreseeable future because of Katrina.

With the flooding of our kids' schools, the bank where I worked downtown, and the downstairs of our home, my family was now one of up to 1 million other south Louisiana evacuees from all walks of life who were now looking for a temporary place to live.[4] Southern Louisiana residents had scattered all over the country, but the largest percentage outside Louisiana—an estimated 250,000 of evacuees—all sought refuge in Houston, Texas.

And Katrina—the most destructive storm in history, covered by news media extensively across the world—perhaps overshadowed the next historical event that would unfold in Houston: "the largest shelter and evacuation operations in American history."

---

[4] The information, direct quotes, and data in this section and the upcoming sections borrow heavily from "Houston's Helping Hand: Remembering Katrina," available in *Houston History* – Volume 7, Number 3, Summer 2010, housed in the Houston History Archives, Special Collections, University of Houston Libraries.

"We're Taking 'Em All"

Two days after the storm, Harris County Judge Robert Eckels was startled awake by a phone call at three o'clock in the morning. On the line was Jack Colley, the State Coordinator of Governor Rick Perry's Division of Emergency Management (GDEM).

"Sorry to wake you up, Judge," Colley said. "But get ready. We're taking 'em all."

It was the second phone call that Judge Eckels had received from Colley that week. Just days before, Colley had called to ask the judge if as many as 2,000 people could be housed in the complex around the Astrodome, the multi-purpose sports dome in Houston and once called the eighth wonder of the world, should the need arise. Like most others in the country, the judge had been watching Katrina intensify in the Gulf of Mexico as it approached New Orleans. The can-do Eckels had told Colley he would "do whatever was necessary to make the facilities available."

Now, with the broken levees and flooding in New Orleans, Eckels would have to make good on his word. Colley asked him to "implement the plan to open the . . . Astrodome to evacuees who would be coming to us from the Superdome tonight."

But this time, Colley increased the number of evacuees who were expected to arrive to a staggering 23,750 people. And Houston area officials had approximately twenty-four hours to make it happen. As *Esquire Magazine* would later tell in its November 2005 issue, the judge said, "'We can do it.' And the race was on."

According to the *Esquire* story, "Eckels instructed Colley to wake up Frank Gutierrez, the county emergency management coordinator, and tell him the ball was rolling. While Eckels worked to get the Astrodome ready, Gutierrez pulled in the Red Cross, which immediately began rounding up staff and tens of thousands of cots and blankets." In an ironic twist, the complex being readied to accept evacuees was managed by sports venue conglomerate SMG, the same company that ran the Superdome, from where the evacuees were fleeing.

The Republican judge then teamed up to oversee evacuation operations with another exceptional political leader, Houston Mayor Bill White. Born in San Antonio to parents who were both schoolteachers, White was a Democrat with non-partisan positions that appealed to his party's supporters as well as Republicans. He had been elected mayor of Houston in 2003. His interest in the welfare of the evacuees from Louisiana went beyond his political responsibilities—his wife Andrea had ties to the neighboring state. Andrea's father was originally from New Orleans and an LSU graduate in mechanical engineering, and her mother was from Baton Rouge, Louisiana.

The mayor had rejected a suggestion by FEMA to herd all evacuees onto a large cruise ship in Galveston. White nixed the idea because of the isolation the people would have experienced. He worried about the emotional trauma people would experience after the initial evacuations were completed. In retrospect, considering the fact that another hurricane would arrive mere weeks after Katrina, an evacuation to cruise ships in Galveston would have been disastrous.

Instead, White marshaled every municipal resource he could within Houston's strong mayoral form of government to create a miniature city. From building showers to setting up children's activity areas to making sure the facilities were safe and clean, White did all of this and more.

Meanwhile, Eckels created a relatively flat, unified incident command center at the Astrodome complex. It counted on officials from the federal government, the State of Texas, Harris County, the City of Houston, and non-governmental organizations. It initially only coordinated major needs like shelter and food, public safety, and public health. But it would later expand as the effects of Katrina lingered and people kept coming to Houston for help. The command structure would expand to coordinate up to 60,000 volunteers who would assist with the housing, education, and job needs that existed.

Early in the planning process, Eckels also realized that a strong communications system would be required to unify people across the city, from evacuees housed in area motels as well as facilities he controlled to local volunteers, citizens, and media. The Joint Information Center ("JIC") was set up in the Astrodome and headed by a public information officer who was in charge of coordinating communications both internally and externally, such as to the news media. Eckels created a telephone system and Internet website that contained "situation reports, press releases, media alerts, and other critical command announcements." The leaders held frequent news conferences to keep the public informed and to share critical information.

As leaders and volunteers scrambled to prepare the Astrodome, Mayor White held an hour-long meeting with other leaders to handle one more order of business. He wanted to put a stop to calling people "refugees" and to come up with a name that would convey respect and compassion for those who had lost everything. Evacuees, refugees, and even more derogatory terms were heard, and White wanted none of it. After a couple of days, White's leadership prevailed, and the term chosen was "guest citizens." He told his leaders and the press that "guest citizens" was what he expected everyone to call those who sought help from Houston after Katrina.

And with that commanding but respectful style, Eckels and Mayor White had prepared the City of Houston and Harris County in a matter of twenty-four hours. Their team was ready.

The Buses are Coming

The first bus arrived at ten thirty the night of August 31. It was driven by twenty-year-old Jabbar Gibson, who had commandeered the vehicle from a school yard, filled it with neighbors, and driven it straight to Houston. It was the first time Gibson had ever driven a bus.

The people were fed and allowed to take a hot shower for the first time in days. They were provided a cot to sleep on and a blanket and pillow. Each person received a "comfort package" from volunteers, a package that included basic toiletry and hygiene needs.

Then dozens of buses followed, unannounced. Each bus was filled with people who were either dehydrated or sick from ingesting floodwater. People were weak, fragile, or elderly. There were drug addicts in advanced states of withdrawal, and everyone else who'd been plucked from rooftops or saved in "rubber rafts, inflatable kiddie pools, and floating hot tubs."

At daybreak on Thursday, Eckels and Mayor White told George Masi, chief operating officer of the county's hospital district, to get ready for a crush of evacuees who were sick. "Prepare a significant humanitarian mission," Eckels told Masi.

Masi commandeered 100,000 square feet of an arena next to the Astrodome and began piecing together what would become known as "Katrina Clinic." The clinic was a state-of-the-art, improvised facility that would later inspire Hillary Clinton to pronounce it a model to be studied for years to come. In less than twenty-four hours, Masi and his staff constructed a fully functional hospital that included general surgery units, prenatal units, pediatric units, and mental-health units. Patients could get x-rays, vaccinations, new eyeglasses, and even wisdom teeth pulled.

Meeting the medical needs of the guest citizens was

a particular challenge, and it fell on Dr. Kenneth Mattox. Mattox is a professor and vice chairman of surgery at Baylor College of Medicine and also the chief of staff at Ben Taub General Hospital. Along with Lt. Joe Leonard of the U.S. Coast Guard, Mattox set up facilities that were essentially large Mobile Army Surgical Hospital (MASH) units. Portable equipment such as blood pressure machines was all on site.

In order to ensure that certain infections didn't spread, officials set up fifteen sinks in a line in the Astrodome. The plumbing was improvised through the use of PVC pipes and faucets that could be turned on with people's knees to control the spread of infections. Crews also installed fifteen portable bathrooms.

And the buses kept coming.

As the population grew in the Astrodome, it became clear that the numbers would exceed the fire marshal's limit of 8,000 people. Mayor White overruled the city fire marshal to allow evacuees into the complex housing in the Astrodome and Reliant Center. The neighboring arena would hold another 4,500 evacuees, and Reliant Center, now called NRG Center, would hold 2,300 evacuees. Eventually, the population would reach 17,500 in the Astrodome complex.

When the numbers continued to build, he made the decision to open the George R. Brown Convention Center downtown, which was located a few miles away. It was prepared to hold another 2,800 more. Under these circumstances, families did what they could to create a home in the crowded facilities. They sometimes put their cots together, turned on their side to secure a little family space. It wasn't much, but it was the closest they could come to a home.

Even with the crowds of people, each family had a uniquely heartbreaking story to tell. Mark Sloan, who coordinated masses of volunteers as the director of Community Emergency Response, recalled the first time he went to the floor of the Astrodome to *Houston History* in 2010.

"It was not what I expected . . . I ran into a four- or five-year-old boy that was sitting on his cot, and I asked him if he came in last night. He said, 'Yes,' and I said, 'Well, welcome to Houston.' I asked him, 'Where are your mom and dad?' He said, 'My dad is getting breakfast.' I said, 'Fantastic.' I asked him again, 'Where is your mom?' He said, 'Well, my dad reached for her, but she went under the water.' . . . I didn't go back on the floor for about four days. I was not prepared for that type of answer."

Meanwhile, the population still grew. It eventually became so large in and near the Astrodome that the U.S. Postal service assigned the area its own zip code. But the sheer enormity of the crowd in need didn't deter Mayor White from serving his guest citizens. The complex provided shelter, health care, childcare, mental health services, housing assistance, travel vouchers and employment services to 27,000 people.

Although the evacuees in and around the Astrodome garnered the most media attention, Eckels and White also helped up to 200,000 more people evacuate to Houston hotels, apartments, rental homes and other shelters. My family was among those that decided the best place for us would be Houston, and we made our first stop there at the only hotel near my office in the Galleria area with an available room large enough to hold our family. We arrived with our two loaded SUVs and a couple of weeks' worth of clothing at the Doubletree Hotel on San Felipe Street.

There was one large group of evacuees who found alternate housing on their own, as reported by the respected demographic researcher and sociology professor Dr. Stephen Klineberg of Rice University's Kinder Institute for

Urban Research. According to an article[5] by Dr. Klineberg, "Many failed to realize that an estimated 15,000 evacuees of Vietnamese descent also fled Louisiana for Houston. With little attention from the media, these newcomers found their way not to the official shelters in the Astrodome or the George R. Brown Convention Center but to the 'Hong Kong Mall' in the middle of the Houston Chinatown that spreads for miles along the Bellaire Strip."

"There, the 60,000 Vietnamese families in Houston quietly absorbed them," Klineberg said, adding a notable observation from a survey of the evacuees. "A remarkable 23 percent of all the Asian-American respondents in the 2006 survey said they had Katrina evacuees staying in their home, compared to 5 percent of all Houstonians."

Even with evacuees spread around in various shelters around Houston, Mayor White was willing to do whatever it took to help. No detail was too small. No guest citizen was beyond reach. I personally witnessed this when I got my first haircut in Houston and paid with a credit card. When the barber asked to see my identification and saw that it was a Louisiana ID, she explained that no sales tax would be charged on the transaction.

It was obvious that Mayor White was running a heck of an efficient machine. And his compassion for New Orleanians seemed to permeate throughout the people of Houston.

My friend, Robin Thompson, still recalls her first glimpse of compassion from ordinary Houstonians. She and her husband had just arrived in Houston, their car packed with items they had brought from home during the evacuation. As they waited in a McDonald's drive-thru to pay

---

[5] Data derived from the research of Dr. Stephen Klineberg, "Four Myths About Katrina's Impact on Houston," Urban Edge, Kinder Institute, August 26, 2015.

for their order, a lady in the car behind them approached their car.

The woman asked if they were from New Orleans. She offered her condolences and invited them to her church, where she said they were serving food and giving away clothes. Robin and her husband thanked her, admitting that clothes were much needed. They had managed to pack a lot of items but not a lot of clothing.

Then the woman walked ahead to the window at McDonald's. She spoke to the cashier at the window before returning to her car, waving with a big smile as she walked past. When they pulled up to the window, the cashier informed Robin and her husband that they did not have to pay. The lady in the car behind them had arranged to pay their bill.

Robin would experience more moments of generosity as an evacuee. But even today, she still gets misty-eyed when she remembers the beautiful smile and the friendship of a woman in the McDonald's drive-thru.

Unprecedented Leadership

The evacuation operation etched out a place in history as one of the greatest humanitarian efforts the United States of America has ever seen. It was unprecedented in its scale. No community had ever had the experience of dealing with more than 200,000 evacuees whose city, homes, and possessions had been destroyed.

The compassionate Houston officials and volunteers didn't have to welcome the evacuees. But they did it anyway because that's the character of the people who live there. As the mayor said, helping all of the evacuees would be "something that was right for our country as well as for our fellow Americans."

The evacuation would not have been a success without Mayor White's support. In "Houston's Helping Hand: Remembering Katrina," a reflection on the storm, White is remembered for his direct and humane approach to the Katrina crisis. He set the tone for all of the volunteers who helped, not only in word but in deed. White would say, "A person at the back of the line seeking benefits needs to know the same information as the guy at the front. We don't want someone waiting to find out they don't meet the requirements. That's not how we do business in Houston."

For his part, Judge Eckels received international recognition for Harris County's response to Hurricane Katrina. The judge would later be described as "an island of competence in the face of catastrophe." In 2005, *Esquire Magazine* named Eckels the "Best and Brightest – Citizen of the Year" for his leadership during the storms. He was later named "County Leader of the Year in 2006" by *American City and County Magazine*.

Eckels attributed the success of the effort to the strong personal relationships within the volunteer community, all of which were forged long before Hurricane Katrina. After all, it was Eckels in 2002 who had launched the Harris County Citizen Corps to "create opportunities for individuals to volunteer to help their neighborhoods prepare for and respond to emergencies by bringing together local leaders, citizen volunteers, and the network of first responder organizations, such as fire and police departments."

More than 60,000 citizen corps volunteers came forward and proved themselves essential to the success of the post-Katrina shelter operations. They came from all areas of the community. They were organized and trained and had already volunteered more than 200,000 hours of community service prior to Katrina. When the initial call for volunteers went out after Katrina, over 1,000 volunteers signed up within the first hour—and they kept coming until the crisis was resolved.

Eckels specifically honored a few volunteer organizations. One in the faith-based community was organized by Dr. Ed Young of Houston's Second Baptist Church. Called "Operation Compassion," it was an interfaith ministry made up of dozens of denominations, and it provided Red Cross training for 43,500 additional volunteers. Those volunteers then produced nearly 90,000 personal hygiene kits for those victimized by Katrina.

Dr. Young's caring and compassion came as no surprise to me. His school would later accept our daughter, Katherine, as a student when we permanently moved to Houston, and I eventually had the privilege of meeting the extraordinary people in his church and school.

But the Interfaith effort did not stop there. In fact, almost every faith-based organization was represented. The Muslims served food on September 11th as a symbolic gesture of 9/11. In all, hundreds of organizations were trained and, according to Jennifer Poston in *Houston's Helping Hand*, included "Adventists, Baha'is, Baptists, Buddhists, Catholics, Charismatics, Church of God, Disciples of Christ, Episcopalians, Hindus, Jains, Jehovah Witnesses, Jews, Lutherans, Mennonites, Methodists, Mormons, Muslims, Pentecostals, Presbyterians, Quakers, Sikhs, Universal Unitarians . . . 629 organizations represented."

Reverend J. Eric Hystad of Second Baptist would later explain, "The fact is that in all of the time that we were there, nobody got sideways about doctrine, about theological beliefs. Nobody got in each other's face about, my church is better than your church or bigger than your church. That was just a non-issue . . . We saw people let down their differences and let down their guards for a higher, more noble purpose."

Other organizations in the faith-based community

were also cited in Eckels' testimony to the U.S. Senate. He noted the efforts of the Houston Area Pastor Council as well as Catholic Charities organizations and Jewish Family Services.

Additional nonprofit organizations played a critical role as well. Anna Babin, president and CEO of the United Way of the Texas Gulf Coast, was new to her position when the storm struck. Yet it soon became her responsibility to coordinate the local Houston charity response after Katrina.

Babin quickly realized those efforts would require an experienced helping hand. She turned to the services of Neighborhood Centers, Inc., a local charity whose roots trace back to 1907, when Alice Graham Baker, the grandmother of future Secretary of State James A. Baker III, and her civic-minded friends formed the Houston Settlement Association to provide "educational, industrial, social, and friendly aid to those within our reach."

At that time in the early 1900s, Houston's population was booming—so much so that it was doubling approximately every ten years—and many of these newcomers settled in the railroad yards and warehouses in the Second Ward. The Houston Settlement Association provided a safe place for those new residents to obtain early childhood education for their children while they worked. To this day, the organization—now called Neighborhood Centers, or NCI—serves mostly immigrant and low income families.

In the wake of Katrina, Angela Blanchard, the president and CEO of Neighborhood Centers, established the "Stay Connected" program–staffed almost entirely by those displaced by the storm–to help fellow storm victims find and stay in touch with scattered family members. One family that benefitted was the Lindsey/Chambliss family, whose story was captured on the front page of the *Houston Chronicle* on September 5, 2005.

The family's ordeal began when Shirley Chambliss

and three of her other family members joined her fiancé, Edgar Ned, on the Claiborne Avenue Bridge after the storm. Edgar had been rescued by boat and taken there after helping to evacuate seventy-five residents from the St. Martin Manor retirement home, where he worked. St. Martin Manor was in New Orleans' Ninth Ward, the city's hardest-hit neighborhood.

Overcome with heat exhaustion, two of the Chambliss family members were taken to Kelly Air Force Base in San Antonio. Eight other Chambliss family members, including Edgar Ned and Shirley Chambliss, were eventually evacuated to Houston but were split up between the Astrodome and the George R. Brown Convention Center.

With the family scattered among three shelters in two cities, volunteers engaged Neighborhood Centers to help reunite the devastated family. Within one week of the storm, Neighborhood Centers brought the family back together at the Brown Convention Center in a very emotional reunion.

The effectiveness of Neighborhood Centers and its CEO, Angela Blanchard, would stay with me. I would later arrange a New Markets Tax Credit financing for NCI for its Gulfton area expansion, the Baker-Ripley Neighborhood Center. Capital One purchased the tax credits in one of the first innovative NMTC financings in the city of Houston.

In addition to the efforts of community organizations, many corporations in Houston also provided support. Jim MacIngvale of Gallery Furniture provided cans of baby formula. Tilman Fertita of Landry's Seafood restaurants provided helicopter support. John Nau and the Silver Eagle beer distributor provided thousands of bottles of water. The list of volunteers, thankfully, was long.

It became obvious in the aftermath of the storm that Eckels and his colleagues had learned valuable lessons from working together during a 2001 disaster: Tropical Storm Allison. Allison allowed them to develop the relationships and complete the emergency preparedness training exercises necessary to handle emergencies. In fact, many have said the humanitarian response could not have happened in any other American city.

Valuable Lessons

Before its well-coordinated response after Katrina, Houston had lots of practice dealing with hurricanes, starting with the worst storm in its history, back in 1900. It had hit Galveston, which lies just south of Houston next to the Gulf of Mexico. The unnamed storm is still known today as the deadliest hurricane in U.S. history. It killed at least 8,000 people and perhaps many more who were carried out to sea and never found. Most of the buildings on Galveston Island were destroyed, prompting the city to begin construction of a massive project on the island—the building of a twelve-foot seawall that increased the elevation of the island by twelve feet.

Since Allison, cities along the United States' coasts like Houston and Galveston have remained vulnerable to storm activity. In fact, the sprawling, low-lying Galveston-Houston area was named the fifth-most vulnerable area to hurricanes and tropical storms by Climate Central in 2012. But one particular storm in 1983 forever changed the way the people of Houston prepare for disaster.

It was with Hurricane Alicia, the fifth-worst storm to hit the Houston area. Frances and I knew it well because we had just arrived in Houston after our honeymoon, having traveled to the city from LSU for our first jobs out of college. My job was with InterFirst Bank in the new InterFirst Plaza at 1100 Louisiana Street in downtown Houston.

On August 18, 1983, Hurricane Alicia struck Galveston and then headed directly for downtown Houston. It was the first hurricane to hit the Texas coast since Hurricane Allen struck in August of 1980. Alicia would be remembered as a storm that shattered many windows in downtown Houston with loose gravel from the roofs of new skyscrapers. Our building at 1100 Louisiana would lose a number of recently-installed plate glass exterior windows. The storm also extensively damaged telephone lines, and we were told that our phones in our new Houston apartment couldn't be installed for several weeks.

In the wake of Hurricane Alicia, politicians and officials examined the destruction, prompting changes to rooftop building codes. They also wanted answers on why Houston was caught flat-footed. On September 23 and 24 of that year, two subcommittees of the U.S. House of Representatives held hearings in Houston. The hearings aimed to examine the primary issues related to the effectiveness of the National Weather Center.

Due to the severe damage, the name "Alicia" was retired in the spring of 1984 by the World Meteorological Organization, and it would never be used again for an Atlantic hurricane. It was the first name to be retired since Hurricane Allen in 1980.

But Tropical Storm Allison was devastating as well, and it was an experience that Eckels said prepared Houston to coordinate the evacuation operation during Katrina. Allison hit the Texas Gulf coast at Galveston on June 6, 2001. Although it never approached hurricane status, the storm was unusual in that it hovered over the region for several days. Houston was inundated with rain, getting as much as eight inches. By the time it moved on, twenty-two people in Texas and Louisiana had lost their lives. Allison proved that storms do not need not be particularly strong to be deadly and destructive.

As documented in *Houston History*, Houston Judge Robert Eckels would later mention in his Senate hearing remarks in the aftermath of Katrina that "our first big test was Tropical Storm Allison. In Allison, we actually had a more difficult test for Houston than the later Katrina event because it was a quarter of a million of our own people that we were taking out of their homes and having to shelter somewhere. They were not in the Astrodome, but we had 100,000 homes under water. . . . It was the largest urban flood in the history of the United States until Katrina came along. . . . We learned a lot of lessons in that."

The Wicked Stepmother

As bad as Hurricane Allison was, there may not be another hurricane season in our lifetime like the one we had in 2005, a year in which three of the six most intense Atlantic hurricanes ever recorded made landfall. On September 20th, just weeks after Katrina, the eighteenth storm—and 10th hurricane—of the season was named. Tropical Storm Rita formed near the Bahamas and moved westward into the abnormally warm waters of the Gulf of Mexico.

If Katrina was the "mother of all storms," then Hurricane Rita was the wicked stepmother. Weather forecasters again commanded the spotlight as Rita intensified rapidly, reaching peak winds of one hundred eighty miles per hour. By now, my family felt like we were on a first-name basis with the Weather Channel hosts.

The consensus was that Hurricane Rita would travel right over the Texas coast toward Houston. At that point, Katrina evacuees in Houston became convinced that they were all cursed. Maybe someone had disturbed the grave of the voodoo priestess Marie Laveau, and she was taking it out on all of us.

The news that Rita was barreling toward us couldn't

have been worse. Houstonians had witnessed the horrors Katrina had inflicted on evacuees, and they didn't want a sequel playing out in their city. Having learned the lesson Katrina taught New Orleans, they got the hell out of town.

Less than three weeks after organizing the Katrina Unified Command, Robert Eckels prepared his own community to brace for a storm even more powerful than Katrina. The reports were grim: The hurricane was headed directly into Houston and Harris County. Eckels again coordinated with Mayor Bill White, who issued an order for 1 million people to evacuate. However, residents throughout the region had Katrina on their minds, and more than 3 million people heeded the call to leave town.

One of those that planned to evacuate was a buddy of mine who came over to our apartment to check on us. He asked me when we were evacuating. When I explained we were staying put, he looked at me like I was the biggest idiot in the world. And maybe I was.

But Frances and I talked it through, and we decided to ride it out. I explained to my friend that we had been on the road nonstop for four straight weeks, and we were bone tired. "If the good Lord wants us this bad, then he can come and get us," I told him.

He asked if we had lost our minds. We said maybe, but we didn't think so.

We explained to my Texas friend that New Orleans is not like Houston. While Houston is exposed, New Orleans is closer to the Gulf, below sea level, and surrounded by levees. Also, Houstonians were not accustomed to leaving town. We had first-hand experience with Louisiana hurricane evacuations and wanted no part of a Houston version. It seemed like everyone was leaving Houston for Rita, and the highways would be a complete mess.

As if by nature, most Texans are brimming with confidence, and he was no exception. My friend looked at me and said, "Bill, don't take this the wrong way, but Texas does things a little differently than Louisiana. We have more highways, and we've really studied how to do this. As long as you leave a little early, Texas won't have the same problems Louisiana had," he explained to me with a paternalistic tone. "Plus, we've learned a new traffic technique that will help the evacuation. They call it 'contraflow' where they turn both sides of the highways around so even more people can get out of town."

I couldn't believe my ears. Like the disease I considered it, contraflow had spread west and infected Houston. I looked up at my cocky Texas friend with weathered, wearied eyes. I tried to explain that he had no idea what he was getting into. The traffic was going to be horrible in every direction. People would be running out of gas on the highway. I explained that most would not even make it to wherever they planned to go.

"People die in contraflows," I said. "Where are you going by the way?"

"We're going to Austin," he replied confidently. I rolled my eyes, wished him luck, and asked him to reconsider. Almost everybody I had talked to in Houston was heading to Austin, like it was an extended summer vacation. "I know it sounds crazy to you, but we're going to hunker down and stay right here," I said.

He shook his head, walked toward the door and made one last appeal. "If you change your mind, you're welcome to stay at my mom's in Austin." I told him we appreciated the offer, and off he went into the Texas contraflow.

The evacuation out of Houston turned out to be the largest in United States' history, even surpassing that of Katrina a few weeks earlier. Between 2.5 million and 3.7 million fled the Texas coast before Rita made landfall. Unsurprisingly, it wasn't long before my buddy called me and conceded it was a mistake to dive into that chaos.

"Well, you were right, my friend," he said. "Three hours on the interstate, and we hadn't made it out of Harris County. We turned around and came back home. We're going to ride it out with you guys."

As I predicted, traffic snarled outbound roads. Cars ran out of gas, of which there was a shortage in the area. State highways gridlocked. The normally four-hour drive from Houston to Dallas took up to thirty-six hours for some folks during the Rita evacuation. And the typical three-hour drive from Houston to Austin took some up to eighteen hours.

Making things even worse, it was excessively hot during the evacuation. The heat and gridlock combined to cause 107 fatalities that were blamed directly on the evacuation, *The Houston Chronicle* reported.

Meanwhile, Rita strengthened as it passed over the extremely warm waters in the Gulf of Mexico. By six o'clock in the evening on September 21, Rita attained Category 5 intensity, the highest classification on the Saffir-Simpson scale measuring hurricane winds. Early on September 22, Rita's maximum sustained winds were up to one hundred eighty miles per hour.

The storm was officially the strongest hurricane ever recorded in the Gulf of Mexico—and it was headed straight for Houston.

We went to bed hoping and praying for the best. We woke up early on the twenty-fourth to a dose of good news and bad news. The good news was that the storm had taken an unexpected turn to the north and was now projected to miss Houston entirely.

But I'll never forget the bad news. The center of the storm reportedly hit land at 7:40 a.m. in Abbeville, Louisiana, where my sister who had taken us in after Katrina lived. The storm would continue on through central Louisiana where my mother-in-law lived in Pineville. The storms weren't just after me, I thought—they were after my entire family.

I frantically tried to reach my sister and wasn't able to connect with her until the following day. Fortunately, she was situated on a high spot. She and her husband were unharmed and their home, which now housed some of the possessions we salvaged after Katrina, suffered only minor damages. There were just a number of downed trees. Thankfully, the same was true in Pineville.

But others had not fared as well. The worst news was that the storm had killed seven people directly and 113 people indirectly. And in the aftermath, our home state and the one that took us in during our darkest hours both took batterings. Rita caused an estimated $10 billion in damages.

In Louisiana, the storm surge from Rita inundated low-lying communities near the Gulf coast, exacerbating damage caused by Hurricane Katrina less than a month prior. It topped levees and pushed water further inland. Lake Charles, where many Katrina evacuees ended up as well, suffered from severe flooding.

Meanwhile, some spots in Texas suffered extensive wind damage. Officials declared nine counties in the state disaster areas. Rita also disrupted electric service for several weeks in parts of both Texas and Louisiana. But even with all of the damage, my family and other Houstonians felt we had dodged a bullet in the most dramatic hurricane season we had ever experienced.

HOUSTON, TX. (Sept. 10, 2005) - The Astrodome and Reliant Center, where 28,000 evacuees were sheltered following Hurricane Katrina. FEMA photo/Andrea Booher. Courtesy of Wikimedia Commons.

HOUSTON, TX. (Sept. 2, 2005) - Cots are set up in the Reliant Center to provide additional housing for people bussed from New Orleans in the FEMA organized program. The Red Cross provided a special package for each cot. Photo by Ed Edahl/FEMA. Courtesy of Wikimedia Commons.

HOUSTON, TX. (Sept. 2, 2005) - Hurricane Katrina survivors sheltered in the Red Cross shelter at the Astrodome reflect on their losses. FEMA photo/Andrea Booher. Courtesy of Wikimedia Commons.

HOUSTON, TX. (Sept. 9, 2005) - Lost children room at the Houston Astrodome. Approximately 18,000 hurricane Katrina survivors that are housed in the Red Cross shelter at the Astrodome and Reliant Center, after evacuating New Orleans. Many are still looking for their loved ones. FEMA photo/Andrea Booher. Courtesy of Wikimedia Commons.

HOUSTON,TX. (Sept. 3, 2005) - Houston Police look at Red Cross lost family members board in the Astrodome, where many families from New Orleans were evacuated and still looking for loved ones. FEMA photo/ Andrea Booher. Courtesy of Wikimedia Commons.

HOUSTON,TX. (Sept. 3, 2005) - Counselors and volunteers help stressed and grief stricken evacuees deal with the trauma of Hurricane Katrina in the Astrodome. Many volunteers provided child care to give mothers a break during the day. FEMA photo/Andrea Booher. Courtesy of Wikimedia Commons.

HOUSTON, TX. (Sept. 5, 2005) - President Bill Clinton greets an evacuee in the Reliant Center at the Houston Astrodome. He and President George Walker Bush were at the Astrodome to announce a new relief fund. In the background holding his jacket is Senator Barack Obama. Photo by Ed Edahl/FEMA. Courtesy of Wikimedia Commons.

HOUSTON, TX. (Sept. 5, 2005) - President George Walker Bush and the daughters of Louisiana Governor Kathleen Blanco talk with displaced families in the Reliant Center at the Houston Astrodome. From left, Karmen, Nicole and Monique. President Bush and President Bill Clinton were at the Astrodome to announce a new relief fund. Photo by Ed Edahl/FEMA. Courtesy of Wikimedia Commons.

HOUSTON, TX. (Sept. 9, 2005) - Oprah Winfrey visits evacuees from New Orleans temporarily sheltered at the Reliant Center in Houston following Hurricane Katrina. FEMA photo/Andrea Booher. Courtesy of Wikimedia Commons.

HOUSTON, TX. (Sept. 19, 2005) - Judge Robert Eckels with a Hurricane Katrina evacuee in the Astrodome. Photo courtesy of Mark Sloan.

HOUSTON, TX. (Sept. 11, 2005) - Louisiana Lieutenant Governor Mitch Landrieu, Harris County Judge Robert Eckels and Houston Mayor Bill White (left to right) join Governor Kathleen Blanco at a briefing in the Reliant Center. Thousands of displaced New Orleans citizens are now at the center in Houston. Photo by Ed Edahl/FEMA. Photo courtesy of Wikimedia Commons.

HOUSTON, TX. (Sept. 14, 2005) - Rebecca Warren and Joseph Smothers, formerly of New Orleans and now sheltered in the Astrodome, are married in center floor. Evander Holyfield gave away the bride. Photo by Ed Edahl/FEMA. Courtesy of Wikimedia Commons.

HOUSTON, TX. (Sept. 7, 2005) - Students register for admittance to the Houston school system. Hundreds of students are being accepted into the Texas system on an emergency basis. Photo by Ed Edahl/FEMA. Courtesy of Wikimedia Commons.

HOUSTON, TX. (Sept. 8, 2005) - Louisiana Elementary school students wave good bye to their parents from their school bus as they leave the Reliant Center for their first day of school in Texas. They are sheltered at the Reliant Center and were evacuated from Louisianna when New Orleans was evacuated. FEMA photo/Andrea Booher. Courtesy of Wikimedia Commons.

HOUSTON, TX. (Sept. 3, 2005) - Volunteers help set up cots at the Reliant Center that is to be used for a Red Cross shelter for Hurricane Katrina evacuees. FEMA photo/Andrea Booher.

HOUSTON, TX. (Sept. 3, 2005) - Counselors and volunteers help stressed and grief stricken evacuees deal with the trauma of Hurricane Katrina in the Astrodome. FEMA photo/Andrea Booher.

HOUSTON, TX. (Sept. 2, 2005) - Residents of Louisiana, who had to flee their homes because of Hurricane Katrina, inside the Houston Astrodome. The residents of Texas have mobilzed a massive relief effort to help the those of Louisiana. Volunteers from a number of agencies were on hand to help. Photo by Ed Edahl/FEMA.

HOUSTON, TX. (Sept. 11, 2005) - Houston Mayor Bill White greets Louisiana Governor Kathleen Blanco as she tours the Reliant Center. Thousands of displaced New Orleans citizens are now at the center in Houston. Photo by Ed Edahl/FEMA.

PART THREE

RECOVERY

CHAPTER 8

HOME AWAY FROM HOME

Wednesday, September 21, 2005
Weeks after the storm

In the weeks following the hurricane, New Orleanians who were scattered around Houston did their best to cope with devastating losses. With so much different now, we felt starved for anything that helped us reminisce about home.

One of our friends, Anne Saporito, told us about the time she was reminded of New Orleans in a Houston Best Buy store. She had just walked in when she noticed a young man with a Saints shirt and the team's famous logo, the fleur-de-lis. Excited about seeing another Saints fan in Houston, Anne immediately yelled out the Saints fans' rallying cry, "Who dat!" The young man smiled and quickly responded with an even louder, "Who dat!" Then, another Saints fan in the back of the store who wasn't even visible joined in with another loud, "Who dat!"

New Orleanians were almost like disoriented songbirds, singing out and hoping for a response from the same species. New Orleans' "Who Dat Nation" had established a new colony, right in the heart of Houston.

A Brotherhood of Sorts

Across town, Frances and I also clung to familiar

glimpses of our community back home. We sometimes experienced them in our local grocery store. Frances joked that her new best friend was the checkout clerk on aisle six because she was from New Orleans.

Whenever she and I needed to pick up a few things—and it seemed we always needed something—we looked forward to inching our way in line toward that clerk. At the end of their conversations, Frances and the clerk always ended with, "Okay, dawlin'." It was a typical New Orleans thing to say, though it may have sounded strange to Houstonians. That little phrase made us feel a little closer to home.

Once, while we were standing in the checkout line, I thought I recognized someone a few people ahead of me. His back was turned, and I wasn't positive who it was, but his outline seemed familiar. When he turned toward me, it dawned on me: It was Bill Goldring, as native a New Orleanian as there was.

Bill's family had deep roots in New Orleans. His father, Stephen, had established a liquor business in New Orleans after prohibition. The company had grown tremendously under Stephen Goldring, and Bill had further expanded the business into a global spirits empire. Bill was wealthy—not just by New Orleans standards, but by global ones. The Goldring family also shared the wealth with New Orleans as he was one of the leading philanthropists in the city. Bill would later be described in a *Times-Picayune* article in May, 2012, as a "giant of local philanthropy whose donations have literally changed the landscape of New Orleans.... Goldring was instrumental in developing two of the city's open space gems: Woldenberg Park along the Mississippi River and, after Hurricane Katrina, City Park's Great Lawn." Yet there he was, standing in the checkout line at Rice Supermarket, buying a mop and a broom.

Bill glanced back toward us and recognized me immediately. He smiled and walked over to say hello. After we both exchanged small talk about our mutual situation, I told Bill my story about rescuing the #100 bottle of Buffalo Trace bourbon. His company, The Sazerac Company, was the owner of the Buffalo Trace distillery in Frankfurt, Kentucky, and it was a big client for Hibernia. Bill chuckled about the story and asked me to send him an email about it. I promised him I would, though I never did.

As Frances and I were walking back to our car, I mused, "Wow, this storm affected everyone in the city. Rich, poor, black, and white. Even a guy like Bill Goldring had to relocate." I was still not accustomed to how much had changed for all of us overnight.

I was reminded of this fact when I knocked on a Houston apartment door late one evening to deliver a package to Ernie Eustis, one of the executives at our bank, and his wife, Dee. Ernie answered, and Dee was right behind him, probably wondering who could be knocking so late in the evening. Ernie and Dee were very well-known native New Orleanians.

Ernie accepted the package, and Dee, always the epitome of southern New Orleans charm, politely asked me if I would like to come inside to their small apartment. I thanked her but declined, and I left thinking how seeing both of them in their new "home" seemed especially out of place to me.

The storm had created a brotherhood of sorts, and anyone with ties to Louisiana was welcome. I recognized the same spirit of tenacious brotherhood when I visited the office of Roy Blossman, an attorney with one of the bank's primary law firms, Carver Darden.

Roy was also one of the smartest lawyers I knew, and I hoped his sharp business and legal mind would help me with a significant problem. I had been traveling between New Orleans and Houston to address my clients' highest priorities, and I scheduled a consultation with him to think through a complicated collateral issue for a client who had been flooded.

I found Roy's temporary office thirty miles away in a shopping center in St. Charles Parish, southwest of New Orleans. The suburban shopping complex was near the Hale Boggs Memorial Bridge that Frances and I had crossed when we saw the Norco refinery flare. His temporary location was a far cry from the spectacular views that were offered by his downtown office in the Energy Centre skyscraper on Loyola Avenue, but it would have to do.

When I entered the building, I saw that all of the partners in the firm had reconstructed their office into one bullpen on the main floor. Everyone was making do with what they could, even some of the most respected, well-heeled lawyers in the city. I looked around and waved to my friends, each manning a phone and busily trying to work on their damaged clients' legal issues in the middle of an open floor.

I realized yet again that this storm's scale of destruction was bigger than anything I could've ever imagined beforehand. As much as there was to do both personally and professionally, people like Roy had no time or mental energy to reflect on what was lost. We were mustering everything we had to prevent businesses and home lives from becoming casualties of Katrina.

Sixth-Floor Solidarity

For the Katrina evacuees in Houston and then, later, the Rita evacuees, our bank at the corner of Bering and Westheimer became the primary Texas evacuation site for our Louisiana employees. There, the most affected employees received significant resources, from worker assistance to temporary living subsidies to outright grants. Hibernia—which would later become Capital One—was Mother Goose to a huge number of people at a time when they really needed it to be that. Most of the commercial banking employees relocated to the sixth floor, making it a home away from home. The refugee bankers moved into whatever areas were available. Many sat at temporary desks and foldout tables in an open space on the sixth floor, sometimes three to a table. This area had a translucent glass front, allowing visitors and other employees to watch the bankers cram in together like cattle in a bull pen, like the one I'd seen at Roy's office. They were furiously working the telephones to help their clients get their lives and businesses back in order.

We called that area the "fishbowl," because the glass provided us little—if any—privacy from the eyes or ears of passersby. Employees from the hall or adjacent coffee room could peer through the glass and witness the frenzied activity going on, with the bankers all thrown in there together.

Some of the many bankers who occupied the fishbowl were Ernie Eustis, Cheryl Denenea, Lisa Glennon, David Maheu, Janet Decha, and Kevin Ward. Many others came and went during this tumultuous period, looking for a place to sit, talk on a phone, or use a computer.

Maybe there really is something to the Japanese method of all working together in a room and not in individual offices. Although all of the bankers were working horrendously long hours to help clients get back to normal and the bank back on track, the stress of the storm brought out the best in all of these bankers. I remember being amazed at what a committed group of people can accomplish by working together on a common goal, no matter how unnerving the circumstances. Many told me they had never in their careers seen bankers work so well together.

On the same floor of the fishbowl was the unofficial "privacy" room, a small, windowless conference room where employees could steal a few moments of private time. There, employees who had lost their own homes and were struggling to get their own lives in order could take a break from helping customers. In the privacy of that little room, they could collect their thoughts, negotiate insurance issues, and talk with loved ones. Dollie, our assistant who had relocated with us, would escape to the privacy conference room on her breaks to call the man she was dating, an orthopedic surgeon who had stayed behind in New Orleans for his patients.

As if our clients and bankers didn't have enough to worry about with the destruction of their homes and businesses, they experienced another major problem. Many customers relied on the U.S. Post Office to receive checks, which went through the banks' automated lockbox system that typically improved the collection and depositing of funds.

But after Katrina, the federal mail system in New Orleans was in disarray. Mail was initially rerouted to Baton Rouge, but issues there forced the mail to be diverted to Houston. Unfortunately, Houston was not faring much better. When Hurricane Rita struck soon after, the postal service shut down its Houston facility. The effects of the two storms drove lockbox receipts down some 70 percent. The post office made things worse by being reluctant to admit the problem and fix it, adding to our clients' cash flow problems and our bankers' headaches.

It was among all of these problems that our bankers reviewed our clients' business plans in the little conference room, trying to present solutions for a steady stream of dislocated customers, highly-respected doctors, lawyers, and captains of industry who had relocated in Houston. Most were in shock that their once-thriving companies were now submerged in water, in complete confusion and disarray. Some had lost nearly everything, and many emotional and tearful meetings were held in that little room.

I used the room to meet with employees on various matters—some business and some personal. One of the personal meetings was with an employee who had lost every possession except for the car in which he had evacuated. His single-story home had been completely flooded, and everything in it was gone—even a second car in the driveway. He didn't have a chance to rescue a few belongings in some Hefty bags like I'd had. It was all gone. *All* of it.

This employee had been working the endless hours logged by many after the storm and had not had time to attend to his own personal and family matters. It almost seemed like he had not set aside even a minute to take inventory of his own personal situation. And he had always been one to contribute to charity drives and provide for his family and others.

At the end of our business meeting, I explained to him that the bank had set up a clothing drive on the eleventh floor of the building and that he should not feel any shame about finding a few items for his children in this time of need. His dire situation must have hit home when I told him about the clothing drive. He never dreamed that one day he would lose everything and be on the receiving end of a helping hand. He buried his head in his hands and wept. On that sixth floor during those days, he was not alone.

Paul Davidson, our city president at the time, and his assistant, Linda Richardson, handled many of these human resources issues we encountered—and there were many. In addition to overseeing the bank's clothing drive, Linda organized hot meals daily for forty-five days for all of the displaced employees in the bank's break room on the eleventh floor. Hibernia paid for all of this.

That was also where volunteers heard some of the saddest stories involving employees whose friends or family members had died during the storm. One lady lost her home and every possession, but she had also lost a close family member.

One after another, tragic stories were told and heard. Some of the victims had dazed looks in their eye, shocked at what had happened. Others explained their hopelessness, looking their listeners straight in the eye with stares at once penetrating and sad, as if they were searching for some kind of answer or comfort that might be inside the person listening to them.

They were looking for hope anywhere they could find it, even if it was from a total stranger. I don't know how priests and doctors and other caregivers find the strength to comfort people during their darkest days. It is an emotionally draining experience.

I'm sure many people are still having difficulties today, even more than ten years after the storm. And I have often wondered how the less fortunate were able to cope without such a benevolent employer as Hibernia.

The Merger

After the aggressive expansion throughout Louisiana in the 1990s, J. Herbert "Herb" Boydstun became the CEO of Hibernia when Steve Hansel retired in 2000. Herb was a Mississippi native and longtime Louisiana banker who had built a community bank in Monroe, Louisiana, that he later sold to Hibernia. With intense blue eyes and a full head of white hair, Herb was a devout Southern Baptist who would lead Hibernia not only in continued community activism and through the Katrina and Rita crises—he also ushered the bank into the next chapter in its history.

While employees were busily repairing their homes and addressing customer issues, Herb and the board of directors worked frantically to salvage the merger between Hibernia and Capital One that had been scheduled for September 1st, three days after the arrival of Hurricane Katrina. On August 31st, the eve of the merger, both companies had announced a seven-day delay "as a result of the devastation and disruption caused by Hurricane Katrina."

During that week, I had received numerous calls from my corporate banking friends around the country checking on me and my family. Every one of these bankers assumed that the merger deal between Capital One and Hibernia just would never happen. They said the devastation and uncertainty was simply too big of a gamble for Capital One to take.

They were right about one thing: The stakes were incredibly high. Capital One was formerly known only as a credit card company, and the acquisition of Hibernia was to be its first true banking acquisition. And although Capital One was a large company, the deal was not small potatoes. Hibernia had a total value of more than $5 billion, and Capital One was about to execute what was by far the largest banking acquisition transaction in the history of Louisiana.

Herb and the Hibernia board were in a very difficult spot. They knew Hibernia might have difficulty recovering from the effects of Katrina if the board chose to go forward alone. After all, the storm had devastated the company's facilities and operations in New Orleans. However, they had a duty to the shareholders, and any renegotiation of the deal would not be well-received.

In fact, according to Randy Howard, the board was worried about potential litigation, no matter the outcome of discussions about possibly renegotiating the merger. If the Hibernia board elected to accept a lower price for the bank, unhappy investors would likely sue the board. But the board would also likely be sued by unhappy investors if it rejected a lower price and elected to remain independent. It was a classic case of being damned if you do and damned if you don't.

Only Herb, Hibernia board member Randy Howard, and a few others know exactly what happened during the tense re-negotiations that occurred during the seven-day postponement of the merger. But on Wednesday, September 7th, before the New York Stock Exchange opened, Capital One and Hibernia announced amended terms for the merger. The deal would move forward, but at a price that was nine percent lower and with a guarantee that the deal would close—no matter what might happen after the announcement.

The stock market responded reasonably well. The Hibernia stock only fell 4.9 percent for that day. In fact, many analysts would report that they had feared the damage to Hibernia was much greater than it must have actually been and were unsurprised at the discount.

And the protections built in for the merger ended up being crucial. No one could have predicted that the enormous Katrina, which devastated the eastern part of the bank's operations, would be followed by an even larger storm, Hurricane Rita, which hit the western side of the bank's Louisiana locations.

As our chief public affairs officer at the time, Russell Hoadley, put it, "It is unlikely any corporate board in recent times has faced the remarkable confluence of business crises and opportunities that converged on Hibernia's directors after August 29, 2005. Besides the obvious and significant challenges surrounding recovery from Katrina ... another hurricane struck at Hibernia's important western front."

As Cathy Chessin, the bank's corporate counsel and corporate secretary, would later recall in an email to me:

"It was extraordinary that the board and Herb were able to keep the merger alive. And also remarkable that notwithstanding the pressure of the merger, they were so responsive to the needs of employees and customers alike. I know that I benefitted from the generous assistance Hibernia offered to displaced employees who had nowhere to live, when one of my sons and I returned to New Orleans in January so that he could complete his senior year at (Benjamin) Franklin High School."

She continued, "Hibernia found housing for us at a hotel downtown, where we stayed for several months until we arranged to move to a friend's undamaged but empty house (since they needed to stay in Houston for the entire school year) for the remaining couple of months until graduation. I will certainly be forever grateful to Hibernia for the services and assistance it provided to me."

The Hibernia board met for the last time on Monday, November 14, 2005, at the Houstonian hotel in Houston, Texas. The directors cast their ballots and made history. The 135-year-old Hibernia that had been started by twelve Irishmen in a law office on Camp Street in New Orleans was sold to Capital One.

The torch had been passed to a relative newcomer, a financial conglomerate that was only seventeen years old. But Hibernia employees did not know that this unfamiliar company would be as good—or better—to the communities it served. Now called "associates," they would soon learn that the company's simply-stated values, "Excellence and Do the Right Thing," were practiced daily.

After the merger, Capital One immediately picked up where Hibernia had stopped. Among its projects was providing stipends to people for temporary housing. And, in May of 2006, Capital One announced a $3 million donation to New Orleans and other parts of Louisiana affected by Katrina and Rita. The bank earmarked the funds for education and the strengthening of nonprofit community organizations.

The company's donation included $1 million to twenty community organizations in New Orleans that addressed affordable housing, education, public libraries, and health and social services. Another $1 million went to ten community organizations throughout Louisiana that provided afterschool or literacy programs benefitting children and their families.

Yet the largest, single award was a $1 million donation to the UNO Charter School network, the entity that Jim Meza, Tim Ryan, and I had started only two years earlier after a couple of beers at a Hornets basketball game.

The turmoil the community experienced after the storms understandably caused many to focus on their own individual issues. Many may not have even seen the extent of the assistance offered to the community by Capital One because of the attention paid to other aspects of the recovery efforts in and around New Orleans. But I was a witness, and so were many other managers like me who personally experienced a company living up to the values it espoused. We watched the bank make a profound difference in the lives of people, customers, communities, and associates at a time when leadership and compassion was exactly what they needed.

CHAPTER 9

A WORLD OF DIFFERENCE

Monday, September 26, 2005
Weeks after the storm

Settling into temporary homes and workplaces wasn't the only challenge faced by New Orleanians. Many of us also lost our churches and schools, including that of my family.

News coverage of a breach at the levee near our St. Dominic Church Parish in Lakeview was broadcast all over the planet. We knew our friends in that community had suffered devastating losses. Still, it was worse than any of us imagined.

When the waters of Lake Pontchartrain had risen with Katrina, a section of levee floodwall along the 17th Street Canal near its mouth had collapsed and caused a catastrophe. The breach occurred on the east side of the levee toward Lakeview in Orleans Parish. The west side of the canal, an area called Bucktown in neighboring Jefferson Parish, did not breach and was mostly dry. This was one of the most significant levee failures that occurred in the wake of Katrina's landfall, contributing to putting the majority of the city underwater.

Large parts of the Lakeview neighborhood became inundated within minutes. Some areas received as much as fourteen feet of floodwater. Near the breach itself, the force of the rushing water uprooted trees and even separated some houses from their foundations.

Almost all of our friends at St. Dominic lost their homes and possessions.

But one thing the storm could not take away was the fighting spirit of the people who built the community into what it was, including the principal of St. Dominic, Adrianne LeBlanc. Ten days after the storm, LeBlanc was determined to visit her school by boat. She launched a boat with her brother Richard from Veterans Memorial Boulevard and the 17th Street Canal, accompanied by three loyal friends and parishioners of the church: Frank Bevinetto, Randy Reboul, and Keith Reboul.

The group found that virtually all of Lakeview, an area with a population of approximately 10,000 residents, was destroyed, including the school and church buildings. There was eight feet of water in the church, and the school took on ten feet. There was no hope of returning to the campus on Memphis Street in Lakeview that fall.

But the resourceful LeBlanc didn't waste any time getting to business. She knew that communicating to parents and teachers of her seven hundred students would be her first task. She directed the boat to the school at the intersection of Harrison Avenue and Memphis Street to retrieve laptop computers from the second and third floors of the campus' buildings, which were still intact.

Soon after collecting the laptops, another loyal friend, Sammy Culotta, set up an Internet connection. More friends, John and Jean Prejean, established a website to collect information on school family whereabouts. When two St. Dominic staff members, Joann Rogers and Tricia Culotta, turned on computers at a temporary office in cramped living quarters they shared with family and friends, emails from parents began pouring in.

LeBlanc responded to the concerns of her student's

families one by one. The New Orleans native who had been raised in a strong Catholic family of fourteen children was bound and determined to pull together the remnants of her community, one step at a time.

A Close-Knit Community

Like Adrianne, Frances and I loved St. Dominic Church Parish and the Lakeview community. Our involvement went back twenty years—when Frances and I had moved to Lakeview back in 1986 on the heels of the oil bust—and we'd stayed involved even after we affiliated ourselves with another parish in Old Metairie.

I remember that the mood in New Orleans was decidedly gloomy back then. The 1984 Louisiana world's fair missed its attendance goals and ultimately went bankrupt. The unemployment rate hovered near twelve percent, and state oil revenues—which made up forty-one percent of state revenues in 1982—had collapsed due to lower oil prices.[6]

Add to all of that the defeated proposal to raise property taxes, and it was no wonder that finding decent homes and schools was difficult for families. But that's what was at the top of our mind, especially since Frances was three months pregnant with our first child, William. We had set our eyes on the close-knit community of Lakeview, an area bounded by

---

[6] When Edwin Edwards took office in the early seventies, he passed legislation tying the oil severance tax to the price of oil, and the money rolled in. In the 1981-1982 fiscal year, 41 percent of the state's revenues came from minerals. Edwards spent this money freely, especially on public employees—Louisiana has more of them per capita than any other southern state—and on pork-barrel construction projects. When the price of oil dropped, however, Louisiana was in trouble. Derived from Nicholas Lemann, "Hard Times in the Big Easy," The Atlantic, August 1987: http://www.theatlantic.com/magazine/archive/1987/08/hard-times-in-the-big-easy/304364/.

Lake Pontchartrain to the north, the Orleans Avenue Canal to the east, City Park Avenue to the south, and the 17th Street Canal to the west. It included the West End, Lakewood, and Navarre neighborhoods, as well as the neighborhoods of Lakeshore and Lake Vista along Lake Pontchartrain.

In the 19th century and early 20th century, that area had been mostly undeveloped swamp. Crews cut the New Basin Canal through the area in the early 19th century. Large-scale residential development, mostly of bungalows, began throughout much of the area after World War II. When New Orleans became a majority-African American city after 1980, Lakeview would go on to remain one of the only almost entirely white neighborhoods remaining in New Orleans. Further, what started as a mostly middle-class section became more economically upscale in the last part of the 20th century, as larger, newer homes were built to replace the earlier, more modest ones that had been there.

Meanwhile, we found our way to St. Dominic Parish, where we found fulfillment in our school and our Lakeview community. We grew to enjoy living there. We had intended to stay for no more than five years, but five years would eventually turn into two decades as we became dedicated members of the St. Dominic Church Parish.

Frances volunteered at St. Dominic and eventually started a Bible school that was in session during the children's summer vacation. St. Dominic later hired her as an elementary education teacher and as coordinator of the liturgical music. In her role as coordinator, she taught the songs at mass for the church and arranged special services for all of the children in the school.

Frances taught thousands of children during her tenure, and she came to be known for the hand motions she used to help the children better understand the songs. The kids called her "Miss Frances," and we couldn't go to a grocery store anywhere in and around Lakeview without hearing a child call out her name.

We had been busy making memories outside the school as well. As William grew older, I would take him over to the Fleur de Lis playground, a popular place for families, children, and people of all ages at the intersection of Fleur de Lis and 40th Street. The playground was built among a grove of live oak trees a block from our first rented townhome on Avenue A.

There, I would chase William around as he played on the monkey bars and slides on the playground equipment. We used to knock the tennis balls around on the tennis court that stood next to the playground, often over the fence and into the street.

But now, in the weeks after the storm, I couldn't believe that the setting for many of my favorite memories had become the veritable theater of nightmares it was during Katrina. Over the years, we had crossed the canal from Orleans to Jefferson Parish hundreds of times via Old Hammond Highway to enjoy a po-boy at R & O's in Bucktown. Our playground was only three hundred yards away from the 17th Street canal breach.

The breach in the 17th Street Canal was primarily responsible for the destruction of Lakeview. Not only did it submerge the Fleur de Lis playground in more than eight feet of water, but it was also the likely source of some of the floodwater that traveled several miles over to Old Metairie and inundated our home on Bath Street. The long established community of 9,875 people and 2,657 families was devastated.

A Man for Others

Now, with our community under water, one of our

first challenges was finding schools for our children. Many parents had no choice but to request refunds of their school tuition from St. Dominic so they could enroll their children elsewhere. But it wasn't always so easy—LeBlanc would have to explain to some that the U.S. Postal Service had somehow lost the tuition refunds in the disrupted mail system. Nonetheless, soon, students had scattered and managed to enroll in other schools across the state and country.

Thankfully, our oldest son, William, was safely away at Belmont University in Nashville for his freshman year. My family only had to find a place for our younger son, eighth-grader Chris, and our daughter, sixth-grader Katherine. Katherine was quickly placed into a Catholic school named St. Cecilia, but Chris' academic situation was slightly more difficult.

Chris had started his eighth grade year a week before the storm at Jesuit High School in the Mid-City part of New Orleans. Because his campus had taken on several feet of water, we hoped to enroll Chris at Strake Jesuit, the largest Catholic high school in Houston. However, Strake Jesuit started at the ninth-grade level and did not have an eighth-grade class. We figured we would have to put Chris in another school, but, the day after the storm, Strake Jesuit's administrators announced that it would enroll and find housing for as many Jesuit students from New Orleans as possible, even the eighth graders.

At first, Strake Jesuit believed it could welcome up to fifty New Orleans students. But the school ultimately figured out a way to accommodate more than eight times that amount.

The thought of adding so many students was naturally daunting for Strake Jesuit.

"I must admit that part of me is scared that we as a community are going to open our doors to whatever members of the Jesuit High School community from New Orleans need a new school," Strake Jesuit President Father Dan Lahart told his students shortly after the storm. "Where will we put them? How will we schedule classes and even lunch? Will they feel part of our community? What will it be like for them to be Crusaders, the mascot of their archrival (Brother Martin High School) in New Orleans?"

Nonetheless, Lahart urged his students to take peace "in knowing that Jesus asks us to care for those in need, peace in knowing that we will be a better community for reaching out."

Lahart's faith was matched only by his charismatic leadership and strong communication. His charm, quick wit, and easy smile conveyed his comfort even in this difficult situation. He would have easily qualified for a corporate CEO job but elected to stand here instead, serving the Jesuit students. He put all of his spiritual and Stanford M.B.A. training to addressing one of the biggest challenges that he and the Strake Jesuit students had ever faced.

Lahart's students heeded his plea, as my son and I would soon discover. And few blessings have been as great for my family.

Looking back, I shouldn't have been surprised. I'd read the mission statement of the school before deciding to enroll Chris there, and if that was an indication of its values, I felt reasonably sure our son would be in good hands during our temporary stay in Houston. The mission statement read:

Since our founding by Fr. Michael Kennelly, SJ in 1960, Strake Jesuit has been educating boys from the Houston area to become Men for Others. Now in our fifth decade, our commitment to excellence is seen in academics and athletics, in our retreat programs and our community service opportunities, in a wide range of extra-curricular activities all designed to help a boy grow to be a responsible man of faith.

While Jesuits have been in Houston since 1960, we have been educating young men worldwide since 1540. For almost five centuries Jesuits[7] have known that education is a key way to serve God's Greater Glory.

Our mission is focused on graduating young men who, through our rigorous training, reflect our ideals of being intellectually competent, open to growth, religious, loving, and committed to doing justice. . . .

This is an extraordinary community made up of students and faculty, parents and alumni. If you are member of this community, you already know that this is a special place. If you are considering joining us, you have some exciting times ahead.

That mission statement was entirely accurate. Not only was that semester full of exciting times, but the community of students, faculty, and parents stepped up to show how truly extraordinary they were—beginning with the way they handled the surge of applicants from New Orleans.

The largest number of relocated New Orleans Jesuit students applied to attend Strake Jesuit after the storm because it was relatively close to their hometown. But too many New Orleans students were interested in temporarily transferring to school, so the matter required some creativity beyond simply absorbing the students into the regular academic day.

Consulting with Jesuit High School in New Orleans, Strake Jesuit devised a "platoon" system that would accommodate all of the students who had evacuated to Houston.

---

[7] The Jesuits are an all-male order of Catholic priests founded by St. Ignatius of Loyola, a Spaniard, in 1540. The order went on to convert millions around the world to Catholicism as well as establish well-respected schools across the globe.

The plan was ingenious. Because Strake Jesuit ended its regular schedule at three o'clock every afternoon from Monday to Friday, the Jesuit New Orleans kids would arrive for a "Second Session" of school and utilize the campus until nine o'clock most evenings. But the guest students' schedule ran from Sunday through Thursday, affording both them and their Houston counterparts full reign of the campus once a week.

A large number of Jesuit New Orleans teachers who had also evacuated to Houston made the plan possible. What's more, the schedule allowed families to return to New Orleans on Fridays to repair their homes on weekends.

The logistics were mind-boggling, but they were no match for Strake Jesuit's administration. The school had no problem organizing a drive for school supplies to benefit its new students. It drew up a registration form and posted the document online almost immediately after it became clear how devastating Katrina had been in New Orleans. It contacted local athletics officials to learn what it would take for the displaced students to participate in sports.

Other Jesuits schools from elsewhere in the country also pitched in, sending money, computers and offers to take in as many students as necessary, Lahart said.[8]

It all paid off. At one point, more than 400 displaced students attended classes at night with the teachers and classmates they would've had back home. The hundreds of new Strake Jesuit students received assistance from the Strake Jesuit Development office team. Some only needed orientation, while others needed counseling and housing. Each of the new students were assigned a "buddy" from

---

[8] In fact, Lahart said, the Jesuit school Regis High in New York City took on its lone Jesuit student ever during this time: a boy that Katrina displaced from Jesuit New Orleans.

the Strake Jesuit student body to help them adjust to their new surroundings.

Further, as Lahart would later announce at a question-and-answer session with parents, the school waived the fees for all of the New Orleans students' uniforms and books. And Strake Jesuit would not charge the new students' parents any tuition for the semester because he knew they'd already paid it to Jesuit New Orleans.

Upon mentioning the tuition waiver, Lahart recalled, parents stood up and applauded.

It was "the first time I've ever made a tuition announcement that was so warmly received!" Lahart exclaimed years later.

Thanks to this school community, our son Chris and I were able to carve out somewhat of a routine that semester. I ate lunch with Chris daily at two o'clock and then dropped him off at school. I'd work later than usual—until 8:45 p.m. or so—and pick him up at nine o'clock for dinner. This was our life for the entire 2005 fall semester, at least on the nights when I didn't have to travel for work.

Even with a tremendously supportive school and schedule, Chris and I still faced difficult logistical challenges. I had to travel a lot during this period, helping clients and the bank get back to normal as well as traveling back and forth between Houston and New Orleans to get our own house in Old Metairie in order. And then in late October, Frances and Katherine moved back to New Orleans before Chris' semester was done, complicating our schedule even more. Sometimes I had to travel for an overnight trip and leave my thirteen-year-old to fend for himself.

Some days I'd get called away unexpectedly, and I'd have to arrange for someone to pick up Chris from school. I'd place notes on our kitchen table along with instructions on what to cook or eat for dinner. I felt particularly guilty a couple of times when I left him over a long weekend. I would leave a nice dinner and dessert behind for him so that he would at least have that when he returned to an empty apartment. "Steak and cake," we would later call it.

But through all of these challenges, I took comfort knowing that Chris was in good hands at Strake Jesuit. The administration supported my eighth grader through a challenging year as he transitioned from middle school to high school, often left alone with few activities other than school and hanging out in an empty apartment.

In an address to the entire student body on September 6, 2005, Lahart talked about all of the changes that had confronted us newcomers. He told them,

> We don't take in these students because it is easy, or fun, or good PR, or even because they'd do it for us. We do it because it is the right thing to do. You will be faced with similar situations often in your own lives. Often. Doing the right thing, even when it is difficult: This is being a 'Man for Others.'

I had heard the Jesuit motto "Men for Others" many times over the years at Jesuit in New Orleans, from which my oldest son William had graduated some four months before the storm. But now, the phrase took on a new meaning for us after experiencing Katrina. I had always thought of this phrase as a way for me to think about others in need. But I never imagined that my family and I would benefit from "men for others."

The term continued to resonate with me as I witnessed the phrase in action on the Strake Jesuit campus. Father Lahart put his school's money where its mouth was, sharing all of the resources at his school's disposal to aid people who had few other options for their boys. I asked Father Flavio Bravo, one of Chris' teachers, if the term had always been a part of the Jesuit doctrine. He advised me that it had a relatively recent history, so I researched the origin of the phrase.

"Men for others" was first found in an address by Jesuit priest Pedro Arrupe to the Tenth International Congress of Jesuit Alumni of Europe in Valencia, Spain, on July 31, 1973. Father Arrupe was the Superior General of the Society of Jesus. At the time, the address—given to a crowd of mostly male Jesuit alumni—caused a stir because some insisted that the objective of a Jesuit education needed to be changed. However, Father Arrupe explained, "To the extent that any of us shut ourselves off from others we do not become more of a person; we become less."

The last paragraph of his lengthy address then read:

Men for others: the paramount objective of Jesuit education—basic, advance, and continuing—must now be to form such men. . . . Only by being a man for others does one become fully human, not only in the merely natural sense, but in the sense of being the spiritual person of St. Paul. The person filled with the Spirit; and we know whose Spirit that is: the Spirit of Christ, who gave his life for the salvation of the world; the God who, by becoming a human person, became, beyond all others, a man for others.

Chris and I realized we were a part of a privileged group, affected in the best way by Father Bravo, Father Lahart, and their administrative colleagues. Sadly, we've since learned that both priests will be moving on to other Jesuit assignments. Father Lahart was tapped to become the president of Regis High School in New York, and Father Bravo has been reassigned to Puerto Rico.

In the spring 2015 issue of *The Chronicle,* President Lahart said of Bravo's departure,

Cura Personalis. This important term from St. Ignatius, translated as "care of the person," is what Jesuit schools are all about. Each of us here at Strake Jesuit, whether faculty or staff, Jesuit or layman, strives to provide personal care for our students. This happens on retreat, but also in the classroom, on the athletic field, through our robust counseling program, and in interactions throughout the day. We all are committed to caring for the individual persons placed in our care. Father Bravo has done an excellent job in modeling *cura personalis* to all of us here at Strake Jesuit during his years with us. This care of others is at the heart of what we desire for all our students as we encourage them to become Men for Others. This is more than a slogan for us, more than a motto. It is our way of proceeding.

Many years later, while reflecting on the post-Katrina semester at Strake Jesuit, Lahart added, "Our decisions were never governed by financial realities; I knew that somehow it would all come out okay."

I couldn't have said it better.

The Lost Children of Katrina

Unfortunately, not everyone was blessed with men who welcomed them into their community or generously shared their resources like Strake Jesuit. Sadly, for some people, their time after the storm was not defined by support and understanding friendships.

New Orleans journalist Katy Reckdahl brought this painful truth to light in an April 2015 article titled, "The Lost Children of Katrina." The article, published online by *The Atlantic,* recounted how the Lee family evacuated to a

Houston neighborhood "so rife with hostility for evacuees that the ice cream truck refused to stop for them." After the initial welcome, neighbors soon believed it was time for the strangers to go home.

The Lee family learned the hard way that the term "guest citizens" that Mayor White had coined did not apply to them. Peers preferred the more derogatory term "refugee" and encouraged the three Lee children to "swim home" to New Orleans to relieve the burden on Houston, said Devante Lee, who was eleven years old during Katrina, according to the article.

Devante, his thirteen-year-old brother Devine, and his fourteen-year-old sister Cessileh were kept home from school by their mother, who feared for their safety in and after school. Devine remembers spending most of the year after Katrina playing basketball on a nearby court. Devante remembers mostly staying at home, yearning to return to New Orleans, the article said.

The Lees' mother did not expect her children to lose an entire school year. But days turned into weeks, and weeks turned into months while waiting for New Orleans to clean up and reopen schools. Then, three months after the storm, Governor Kathleen Blanco announced that the state would take over public schools and hand them over to charter school operators, similar to the New Beginnings charter school that Jim Meza had pioneered.

"Parents have new expectations for what schools should be . . . and families will only return home when we can meet these new, and higher, expectations," Blanco stated. The Lee family was caught between a Houston neighborhood that didn't accept them and a New Orleans school system that wasn't ready to take them back.

When the Lee family did return to New Orleans about a year after the storm, what they found was disappointing. According to the article, classes were taught in temporary buildings by interim teachers and were sometimes shut down without notice.

It was all grueling for the Lees. They had lost everything in the storm. Their mother found a new place when they returned to New Orleans but "worked three jobs to pay the rent, which had doubled due to the lack of housing," the article said. At night, Devante remembered she would "come into their room, give us a kiss on our foreheads, and say a little prayer. She'd kiss and pray."

According to the article, when Devonte thinks back, "he wonders about how his life would be different if he'd had a normal high-school experience, with stable teachers and classmates by his side for years. But he stops short after a few minutes, as if he's unable to go any further. For him, he says, the year that Katrina happened basically doesn't exist. He believes that others his age also avoid looking back. "People are blocking it out of their minds," he said. "I don't like to think about it too much myself."

In reading about the Lees' experience and about many other children whose education was neglected during this time, I realized how many families would have loved to have a school like Strake Jesuit to help look after their children while the parents did what they had to do for work. Strake Jesuit spared us from a bad experience by wrapping their arms around my son at a time when we both sorely needed that. Neither Chris nor I will ever forget that, fully aware that others were not as lucky.

Silver Linings

Later that semester, Chris and I received word that Jesuit New Orleans was ready for its students and faculty to return to its campus. Under the leadership of its president,

Father Anthony McGinn, Jesuit became the first flooded school in New Orleans to reopen.

The reopening of the campus was a victory in itself. However, an even more meaningful victory awaited the faculty and students who would return in time for Thanksgiving. Despite the challenges of that fall, the school still held its annual Thanksgiving Drive, in which students delivered meal baskets to needy families in the area. It would now be the Jesuit student body's turn to again be "men for others" in New Orleans.

So, after Chris completed his fall semester at Strake Jesuit, I packed the Expedition up, picked him up from school, and with him said goodbye to Houston. Along with many other New Orleans families who took shelter in Texas, we headed back to the Crescent City on the familiar artery, Interstate 10, which had been the site of the contraflow traffic plan that had been executed just a few months earlier.

It was the last of many road trips we'd taken along that highway between New Orleans and Houston during that semester. I have fond memories of those trips. Many fathers grumble about not being able to communicate with their teenagers. But an unintended benefit of the storm was that the trips—though we loathed them—provided plenty of opportunity for us to talk about any number of topics. I had my son confined alone with me in a car for six hours, and he had no choice but to endure my fatherly intrusions into his school and personal life.

While driving back along I-10, we noticed many other Louisiana license plates on cars loaded with families headed back home with their possessions. Several of these vehicles sported new bumper stickers that had become popular after the storm and read, "THANKS HOUSTON." Nearly everyone I knew who evacuated to Houston shared these sentiments. We all knew that we had benefited from an unprecedented humanitarian effort.

On that final drive back to New Orleans, I asked Chris whether the storm had been a good or bad experience for him. He paused for a bit, and then he said, "Well, losing my home and my city was no fun. But this did give me an opportunity to meet some new people and experience a different city."

We talked about how impressed we both were with Strake Jesuit—and we knew our gratitude was shared by New Orleanians and Houstonians alike. Many friends had told me that this experience may prove to be a defining moment in the school's history, up there with any sports trophy captured or academic achievement experienced by the institution. That's because—aside from sharing their campus—many of the students hosted New Orleans kids at their families' homes. As a result, many friendships formed during that time endure to this day.

Then Chris said, "And . . . well, Dad, I think you and I became even closer together. So, while it was a bad thing, some good things came out of it."

I can't describe how happy I was to hear that Chris hadn't minded our long car rides together—and that he even felt the same way about our becoming closer. Our memorable conversations became a silver lining in the clouds that hovered over us in the days after Katrina struck.

Thanks Houston

With all that said, there was an uglier side to the Houston evacuation. The strain that Houston felt while accommodating so many newcomers was beginning to show toward the end of our stay there in the fall of 2005. That's when some in Houston began questioning the sincerity of the "THANKS HOUSTON" message. Skeptics believed the bumper sticker was thinly veiled sarcasm, an expression of feigned gratitude to Houston because the city had transferred a hundred thousand poor people to Texas. Personally, I firmly don't believe this was the case. These skeptics were simply upset—understandably so, in my opinion—when an increase in certain types of crimes in Houston was reported following the evacuation.[9] I understand the skeptics. But I recall that these bumper stickers and signs emerged well before any crime increase was mentioned by the media, and they were simply a genuine gesture of appreciation.

Even today, many Houstonians openly claim that New Orleans evacuees were responsible for an increase in crime in the city and lament the city's acceptance of evacuees and helping hand. Some other residents blame every malady that Houston has suffered on the evacuees, including the city's traffic woes. Local radio shows fanned the flames of such negativity—I suspect because the hosts believed it helped ratings.

Still, I find that some who criticize Houston's response after Katrina don't tell the whole story. They fail to mention that there were tangible benefits that Houston received from some of those who were displaced after Katrina.

As a banker, I was well positioned to understand some of these positive impacts on the city. And I know of at least ten companies—major ones that were both privately run and publicly traded—that moved their headquarters or a significant number of employees from New Orleans to Houston after Katrina.

One of them was Seismic Exchange, Inc. (SEI), the country's largest owner and marketer of seismic data for

---

[9] That said, during the same time periods, other types of crimes stayed at the same level or saw a reduction, according to numerous reports.

the oil and gas industry, led by its chief executive and chief financial officers, John Havens and Jud Grady, and Executive Vice President Rivie Cary. Mr. Havens has the distinction of being the number two owner of the Houston Astros, behind majority owner Jim Crane. John, Rivie, and Jud also support many Houston charities.

I'm reasonably sure that John, Rivie, Jud, and my numerous other transplanted friends have yet to commit any crimes in Houston. In addition, hundreds, if not thousands, of other Louisiana professionals moved to Houston after the storm. I've never taken the time to research exactly how many new property taxpayers Houston gained from New Orleans as a result of Katrina, but my guess is that it's a pretty big chunk, at least if the amount of LSU bumper stickers and license plates I see around Houston these days are any indication.

None of these boosts should be ignored, even if some out there would prefer to perpetuate the myth that trouble was all that New Orleanians brought to Houston.

Father Dan Lahart and Father Anthony McGinn during registration at Strake Jesuit for the New Orleans Jesuit boys. Photo courtesy of Strake Jesuit, 2005.

Father Lahart addressing the New Orleans Jesuit boys with Father McGinn taking notes. Photo courtesy of Strake Jesuit, 2005.

Father Anthony McGinn of New Orleans Jesuit addressing his students at Strake Jesuit. Father Dan Lahart is seated behind him. Photo courtesy of Strake Jesuit.

Father Anthony McGinn addressing the students at Strake Jesuit. Father Lahart is seated behind him. Photo courtesy of Strake Jesuit.

The New Orleans Jesuit students and their parents gathered to listen to the address from Father Anthony McGinn of New Orleans Jesuit and Father Dan Lahart of Strake Jesuit. Photo courtesy of Strake Jesuit.

Registration Instructions for 8th and 9th grade New Orleans Jesuit students registering for classes at Strake Jesuit. Photo courtesy of Strake Jesuit, 2005.

A T-shirt custom made for New Orleans Jesuit students including the names and school colors of both New Orleans Jesuit and Strake Jesuit. Photo courtesy of Strake Jesuit, 2005.

New Orleans Jesuit students lining up before classes begin at Strake Jesuit. Photo courtesy of Strake Jesuit, 2005.

New Orleans Jesuit students going to night classes at Stake Jesuit. Photo courtesy of Strake Jesuit, 2005.

New Orleans Jesuit student receiving help from his Strake Jesuit "buddy."
Photo courtesy of Strake Jesuit, 2005.

New Orleans Jesuit students meeting their new Strake Jesuit classmates.
Photo courtesy of Strake Jesuit, 2005.

Nunzio J. Santarcangelo (N.J.) at left coordinating the introductions of New Orleans Jesuit students to their new Strake Jesuit buddies. Photo courtesy of Strake Jesuit.

A New Orleans Jesuit student wearing a Metairie Baseball shirt attending an orientation at Strake Jesuit. Photo courtesy of Strake Jesuit.

Strake Jesuit Mothers Club preparing supplies for New Orleans Jesuit students. Photo courtesy of Strake Jesuit, 2005.

New Orleans Jesuit parents and students gathered at the Parsley Center at Strake Jesuit. Photo courtesy of Strake Jesuit.

New Orleans Jesuit students and parents gathered at the Parsley Center at Strake Jesuit. Photo courtesy of Strake Jesuit.

Uptown New Orleans: signs for the 1 year anniversary of Hurricane Katrina thank organizations, volunteers, and cities that helped in the aftermath of the disaster. Photo by Infrogmation. Courtesy of Wikimedia Commons.

NEW ORLEANS, LA. (June, 2008) -- The USS New Orleans (LPD-18) passes by downtown New Orleans on the Mississippi River. The Hibernia tower is shown in the distance. Courtesy of Wikimedia Commons.

Photograph of the Hibernia Tower next door to the New Orleans downtown offices of Capital One. Photo from Wikimedia Commons.

2007, French Quarter, New Orleans. View up Bourbon Street during mid day. This area active catering to tourists at night restocks with delivery trucks during the day. At night this is a pedestrian mall closed to auto traffic. In the distance, Central Business District buildings across Canal Street; dome of Hibernia Bank tower visible. Photo by Infrogmation. Courtesy of Wikimedia Commons.

CHAPTER 10

RETURNING HOME

Wednesday, September 28, 2005
Weeks after the storm

As much as we appreciated Houston, the spirit of our school and community back home was too powerful to ignore. During that fall semester when Chris attended Strake Jesuit in Houston, I also worked to get our home back in Old Metairie back to normal. The list of things needing to be cleaned and fixed before my family could move back in was endless, including carpet and sheetrock that needed to be removed and ruined furniture that needed to be thrown out. Thankfully, my Cajun brother-in-law, Jimmy, helped me in those early, torturous days. He's one of those guys that knows a little bit about everything and possesses a specialized tool to fix pretty much anything.

So, as soon as our routines had been established at work and school, I had developed a routine for tackling repairs back in Metairie. I managed work in Houston until Friday afternoon, and then I'd leave to oversee the renovation of our home during the weekend. The first few weeks of this schedule in September and October were horrendous.

Unfortunately, finding qualified contractors to do the work of renovation was even more challenging. Most were overwhelmed with work demands and refused to commit to deadlines, so the jobs fell mostly on the homeowners.

The only reliable choice for homeowners was to do the work themselves or secure and personally monitor the services of various handymen where necessary.

So, in addition to juggling work and the kids, I did the work in Old Metairie either myself or with helpers on Saturday and Sunday. I'd then develop a work list for my helpers for the upcoming week before returning to Houston on Sunday night. It was, no doubt, a grind.

Out on a Limb

One of my helpers was my yard man, Robby. Robby had been maintaining our yard for many years. He worked hard. He was reliable, honest, and reasonable. That is, he was reasonable about most things. As I discovered on one of my trips to New Orleans, Robby did not quite understand his limitations.

I had asked Robby if he thought he'd be able to remove the felled tree in my backyard. I knew Robby was an excellent yard man, but I wasn't sure about his proficiency in the more specialized field of tree removal. While examining the tree with him, I explained the job's complexity. "Do you see how the tree has fallen between this grove of other trees and has not hit the ground?" I said.

Robby said he saw it, and I told him to look at it carefully because the tree was wedged into the others. It wasn't completely severed at the base, and Robby needed to start cutting at the top of the tree because beginning at the bottom where it broke would cause the trunk to snap back at him as soon as he finished cutting, I explained.

"I see it, Mr. Bill," Robby said.

Just to make sure I had been crystal clear, I walked with Robby to the top of the tree to point out exactly where he needed to start sawing and again explained why.

"I see it Mr. Bill," he replied for the third time. "I've been doing this kind of work for a long time. Don't you worry about a thing, Mr. Bill. I even got a John Deere tractor and everything."

I didn't understand why a tractor was relevant to the job at hand, and it was clear that Robby was venturing into unfamiliar territory. But I was exhausted from working on the house all weekend, so I just said, "Okay, Robby. I'm going back to Houston. But please take care of the tree this week, okay? And please be careful."

Robby said, "Don't you worry about a thing, Mr. Bill."

With that, I got in my car and started the long drive back to Houston. I worried about how Robby would saw that tree up during the entire trip.

Five days later, at the end of the ensuing work week, I left Houston earlier than usual and arrived at the house late one afternoon. I walked to the back of the yard and realized that the tree for some reason had not yet been removed. Robby's tools were strewn about the yard. A chainsaw lay under the tree. And the shiny new John Deere tractor was parked nearby. The scene was strange to me because Robby was always so neat with his tools and very particular about where they went. I wondered why he left them just lying about in the yard.

Then, I heard a voice behind me say, "Mr. Bill."

I turned around to see Robby walking up the driveway toward me. He had on a hospital gown as well as a bandage wrapped around his head. He was short and stocky, so the hospital gown almost reached down to his ankles. I could see that he was wearing boots, but I don't think he had anything else on under the gown.

"Mr. Bill, I guess you heard what happened," he began.

"No Robby, I just got here," I said. "What happened to you—and your head? Are you all right?"

"I'm fine, Mr. Bill. I'll be fine—no problem," he said.

"You see, Mr. Bill, this tree was all bound up in this other tree and, well, I got up on top of the trunk of the tree and started my saw—"

I stopped him there and said, "Robby, you started at the base of the tree? But didn't we discuss beginning at the top of the tree?"

"Yeah, well, yeah . . . I remember," he said. "But anyway, when I started cutting I was doing pretty good, and then, man, that sucker snapped and popped back up and throwed me and the chainsaw up in the air."

Shocked, I asked him what happened next.

"Well, I don't really know," he said. "I guess I got knocked out or something and they took me to the hospital."

I didn't know who "they" were, and I never found out. Robby kept explaining, but I hardly listened. I didn't know whether to hug him or yell at him. I decided not to hug him in case he was as naked under the gown as I surmised he might be. In fact, when he gestured and pointed as he spoke, I remember hoping he didn't expose more of himself out the back of the gown than I wanted to see.

I didn't yell at him either. It just wouldn't have been right to do that to a man with a bandage on his head.

"Robby, did this all happen today?" I asked, strategically turning my body from the more revealing parts of the gown.

"Oh, yes, sir. Today after lunch," he said. "But don't you worry, Mr. Bill. I'm gonna start right back up now and get this tree out of here for you."

"Nonsense," I said. I told Robby that he needed to go home, rest for a while and make sure he was okay. Robby assured me he was fine, and we agreed that he could come back the next day.

The whole experience summed up how absurd things could get for homeowners who were affected by Hurricane Katrina and left to their own devices to repair their family's houses. And we couldn't make up the setbacks that we had to deal with on any given day because help was already hard to come by.

So, I did the only thing I could do in that moment. I went back to my back porch, opened an Abita beer, and thanked the good Lord that Robby had not been hurt worse than he had been.

Gone

Meanwhile, I hoped I could use a bicycle I had previously bought Chris as well as a Virgin Mary statue that belonged to Frances to infuse some much needed joy into my family. But that bike and statue each nearly crushed my spirits.

For many weeks after Robby's accident, I followed the routine of traveling back and forth between Houston and New Orleans to coordinate work with helpers and contractors. I elected to go by myself so that Frances could focus on managing our Houston household, including helping the children complete their homework and getting to their extracurricular activities. Frances and I also had decided that we wouldn't show the kids the home again until we had at least completed the initial cleanup. I wasn't sure if this was the best approach, but the bottom line was we didn't want them to experience the pain we had felt.

During any rare down time I had on those long, lonely weekends in Metairie, I decided to try to repair a couple of personal items for Frances, William, Katherine and Chris. I began by cleaning Frances' statue of the Virgin Mary and placing it back where Frances had put it, in what was left of the backyard garden.

For Chris, I wanted to do something similar: I cleaned and repaired a bicycle that I had given him as a birthday present a year earlier. It was a nice blue, ten-speed mountain bike. Part of it was stained after being inundated in muddy brackish water for ten days, and the lower part of the bike had rusted.

I knew it'd be an involved job cleaning it up, but I saw how Chris enjoyed riding the bike, and that made it special to me. So every weekend, when I returned to New Orleans, I spent the last hour or two of daylight scrubbing and cleaning the bike because I couldn't wait to see Chris ride it again.

That was how my life went for several more weeks. Finally, after about six weeks of traveling back and forth between Houston and New Orleans on weekends, I had cleared the house and yard of trash, debris, molded sheetrock, downed trees, and flooded furniture. The neighborhood was still not at all what my kids had seen just two months before, but it was much better than it had been after the storm.

The weekend before, I had personalized the house as much as I could, placing Frances' Virgin Mary statue back in its rightful spot and leaning Chris' bike—which was in nearly new condition—up on the back porch. I arranged Katherine's bedroom upstairs just as if she had never left. And, with that, Frances and I felt safe bringing the children back to the house, which we didn't want to do too early after the storm.

Still, as we made the drive back with the kids, I could see in the rearview mirror how shocked they were at the appearance of the neighborhood. Our children had kept up with the Katrina events through the extensive television news coverage, but they hadn't yet realized the impact of the storm on our neighborhood and our home. Despite all of the weeks of work, the area remained a mess.

As we approached the front door, I did my best to prepare the kids to see something much different than the home they knew. The outside didn't look much different, but the inside of the house was nothing like they remembered. I explained that it was as if "the guts had been removed."

The house we entered was unfurnished. The barren structure had no carpet, sheetrock, appliances, paintings or anything else it had before the children left. The downstairs was stripped to the studs and the concrete slab. Even the ceiling was gone. I waited for a while until the kids' shock subsided to explain to everyone that I did have a little surprise for each of them, that I had managed to salvage a couple of things which would help them remember the home we had.

At least I thought I did.

I walked to the back of the house and opened the back door. We walked out to the porch where I had placed Chris' bike the weekend before. Anticipating a joyous scene, I asked Chris to walk outside with me to see what I had for him. But then I turned the corner—and the bike was gone. I began saying something to Chris but stuttered. Panicked, I walked to the side of the house to see if it was there, but it wasn't.

"It's gone," I said in disbelief. "It's gone." I said that over and over as I looked around.

Chris didn't understand. "What, dad?" he asked. "What are you looking for?"

But I was stunned silent. Someone had stolen his bike, the one I had spent the last six weeks repairing.

"It was your bike, son," I said. "It was your bike."

I tried to talk. "I had worked on your bike for weeks, and had it good as new, and . . . and . . . somebody must have stolen your bike, son. I'm sorry. I'm so sorry, son."

Chris sensed how devastated I was. "That's okay, dad," he said. "I figured I had lost it anyway. Don't worry about it."

I collected myself and turned my attention to Frances' surprise. I gazed to where I had placed the statue, toward the back of the yard. Lo and behold, it, too, was not there.

"Your Mary," I said to Frances, with the disappointment in my voice obvious. "Your Virgin Mary statue. It's gone, too."

I went back into the house and took inventory. I realized

looters had helped themselves to other items throughout the house: our dining room chairs, flower vases, and decorative pieces Frances kept on the kitchen windowsill.

The shock faded into sadness. But then the sadness turned into anger. I felt the kind of anger that can take a man to a very dark place. What else could I do? What Katrina hadn't destroyed, the looters were taking.

The Looters

I had heard that looters could be quite clever. A contractor explained to me that thieves would enter unoccupied homes during the day and place items they wanted on debris piles out front, as if it were trash. At night, they would drive their trucks down the street, stop at the debris piles, and collect their booty. If they were caught pilfering it, they would simply explain that they were trying to help homeowners remove debris. Their theft was easier than it otherwise could have been because, like us, many homeowners were living elsewhere and were unable to defend their property.

I had also heard that many residents across the area had been victimized by rampant looting in the first week after the storm. It had become so bad that, a few days after the storm, Governor Blanco issued a warning that the National Guard was authorized to shoot rioters and looters.[10] At the time, I thought this was an outrageous overreaction. But later, as a looting victim, I better understood why she issued her warning.

The looters took more than the bike and our Mary that

---

[10] Information derived from James Joyner, "Katrina: Governor Orders Troops to Shoot and Kill Looters," Outside the Beltway, September 2, 2005: http://www.outsidethebeltway.com/la_governor_warns_troops_will_/.

day. They took a piece of our family as well. Until that point, I had generally avoided feeling anger after Katrina. I was so busy trying to repair things at home and at work that I simply didn't even have time to think about being angry.

But that changed when the looters intruded my home. I simply couldn't comprehend how someone would loot a destroyed home of the few possessions a family managed to save. That day, for the first time since Katrina destroyed the region, I became enraged.

It wasn't the loss of the raw possessions themselves. Possessions didn't mean as much to me after the storm. Much of what we lost was stuff I learned I didn't really need. But among their loot were a few possessions with a special memory attached, and those did mean something to me. They were reminders of the peaceful and happy life we had created in our little corner of Old Metairie.

Chris and I had frequently ridden our bikes together on the weekends. We had blazed our own path through the Labarre Business Park to get to the Mississippi River from our home. Once atop the river levee, we would ride downriver several miles to Audubon Zoo in Uptown New Orleans. On the return trip, we would take a winding path back through Uptown on St. Charles Avenue, stopping for snowballs or visiting with friends who lived around there.

The rides would take most of an afternoon, so we called them our "power rides." That was our own special term for our personal adventures, those long, bold rides that sometimes led us through neighborhoods in New Orleans that were more rough-and-tumble than ours. We both felt like actual adventurers in the wild as we navigated any unfamiliar areas we encountered along the way. Our power rides exposed us to parts of New Orleans that few people we knew ever saw.

I was quiet the rest of the day as we picked up bits and pieces of our things and put them back where they belonged. The anger and exhaustion that were brewing were a bad combination. I had always wondered how people got themselves enraged and violent, but that night, I finally understood how it can happen. I don't condone going to such extremes, but I now appreciate how a series of unfortunate circumstances can make a man feel a sense of outrage. The looter had fully prepared me to exact the vengeance I wanted on him.

Both the looter and I were lucky that he never tried to come back to our home.

A Little Louisiana Ingenuity

Our little family wasn't the only one traveling back and forth between New Orleans and Houston, working hard to repair our home. There were many, and each clamored to reunite with their various communities. So, naturally, we were excited to receive a letter from St. Dominic Principal Adrianne LeBlanc, dated October 11, 2005, not even forty-five days after the storm.

She wrote:

Dear Parents,
As we enter the next stage of returning to normalcy now that the city has allowed us all to begin the mammoth task of rebuilding our homes and lives, I hope this letter finds you well and adapting to your circumstances. It has been wonderful seeing so many of you since I have returned to the metropolitan area. I am grateful for your patience, support, and encouragement as we enter the unknown realm that lies before us.

Good news—great news—at least for those of you who have been awaiting the resurrection of St. Dominic School! Plans are progressing quickly, and we will soon be opening a satellite school at the Holy

Rosary School facility. A date? I knew that would be your first question. At this time, a firm date has not been set, but, I assure you it will be as soon as possible depending on how quickly the loose ends can be tied up . . . the dream will become a reality in the near future.

We must all be ever grateful to the Archdiocesan staff, Holy Rosary parish's pastor, Father Tarantino, his administrative staff and the Holy Rosary staff for allowing us to utilize their building while they are relocated for the remainder of this school year. This kind act will work wonders for our children, you, their parents, and the St. Dominic faculty in our efforts to return some semblance of the life we had come to know and love.

If any of you have viewed the St. Dominic facilities, you surely recognize the monumental task we have before us. If you were in the neighborhood today, you may have noticed members of the National Guard helping out with the hard work of restoring our school to its pre-Katrina condition....

Remember that you and your children are in my prayers each day. I look forward with great antic-ipation to reuniting with all of you and working with your children in our new temporary location very soon.

Sincerely,
Adrianne LeBlanc

As the school staff worked feverishly to prepare the satellite school, the St. Dominic community planned its first post-Katrina gathering several days later. There was a Sunday Mass on October 16th at Holy Ghost Church in Hammond, Louisiana, some thirty miles away from St. Dominic's campus. In Hammond, LeBlanc discussed her plan to reopen the school campus of Holy Rosary Academy on Esplanade Avenue to house St. Dominic students for the remainder of the fall semester.

It was about a week after that when Frances told me

she was moving back to our home with our daughter. She had resolved to live upstairs while the downstairs was being renovated. Frances couldn't stand the thought of looters rummaging through our remaining possessions upstairs, though in those days there was really no way to fully patrol your home unless you hired a full-time armed guard, which really wasn't feasible. Regardless, Frances and Katherine also missed St. Dominic.

"But it's not safe, and the rest of the neighborhood isn't back yet!" I protested.

Frances didn't waver. "I'm going back," she said, "and Katherine is going with me. I know you and Chris have to stay for work and school, but I miss my home—what's left of it—and I'm going back."

We argued about her plan for at least a week thereafter, but she prevailed.

"You're a hard-headed woman," I said when I conceded defeat.

"You knew that when you married me," she countered.

And that was that. Whether I liked it or not, Frances and Katherine lived alone upstairs in Metairie for at least two months while Chris and I stayed behind in Houston until Chris finished the fall semester. At least our neighbors behind us in Metairie, Robert and Madeleine Leithman, had also moved back into their upstairs, so Frances and Katherine weren't completely alone.

The Leithmans lived directly behind us, and our families were very close. We were both pioneers of sort in the rapidly developing neighborhood, each having built a two-story house among smaller single-story ones. One day, not long after we moved in, I heard a noise coming from our back yard. My new neighbor Robert Leithman was disassembling our back fence and constructing something. When I asked Robert what he was doing, he replied, "I'm building a gate. I'm tired of walking around the block to visit." That's just how Robert rolled, and we and our families used that gate many times over the years.

For that first month my wife and daughter were back, they joined my backyard neighbors as the only residents of our 200-plus home subdivision. At night, our house lights shone as if they were campfires ablaze in the boonies.

Frances did have my shotgun with her, the one she had become acquainted with on our trip down from Abbeville a little bit after the storm. She kept it leaned against her bedside table so it was within easy reach. Thankfully, she didn't need it. And thank goodness that the looters did not appear again—there's no telling what punishment they would have been in store for had they crossed Frances.

Meanwhile, Adrianne kept her word. St. Dominic reopened at the campus of Holy Rosary just 10 days after Adrianne mailed her letter to parents. It had one hundred thirty-nine students as well as thirty teachers and staff members, including Frances and Katherine.

Week by week, the numbers grew. Within a month, enrollment was at one hundred ninety students. And Adrianne expected the ranks to keep swelling—to nearly three hundred students by January 3rd, when the school would reopen after Christmas.

Just days after Thanksgiving, on Sunday, November 27, 2005, St. Dominic Church held its first post-Katrina Mass. It became clear that the maintenance crews were as resourceful as Adrianne. In a demonstration of Louisiana ingenuity, the maintenance manager, "Mr. Timmy," and three of his colleagues had scrubbed the floors with hot water heated on a crawfish burner.

They, along with the National Guard, had also removed the pews, but no one minded. The church was filled with people either sitting in folding chairs or simply standing. They all yearned for a piece of the life and community they once had—and wanted back badly. Adrianne greeted the parishioners and explained that the school had reopened on October 26th, exactly two months after the last day of classes before Katrina.

Some of that same ingenuity was working its magic in our home as well, which I discovered when Chris and I came home to Metairie after he completed his semester in Houston that December. Though our home was still badly damaged, it was at least now under renovation by a real contractor. Even better, we were happy to be reunited with Frances and Katherine.

Frances loves to cook, and she had prepared a welcome-home dinner for us. But because our appliances downstairs did not survive the flood, Frances had set up a makeshift kitchen out of our hallway upstairs. She had everything from Crock-Pots to portable ovens to waffle irons up there.

Just because we weren't in an actual dining room didn't deter us from going all out for meals. We covered a temporary dining table set up in the bedroom with a white cloth and lit some candles. We ate the pot roast and vegetables she made for us for our first night back, a meal that tasted as satisfying as anything I've ever had. I couldn't have dreamed up a better homecoming.

As more of our neighbors returned, we had more of those small dinner parties right there in our bedroom. The unorthodox setting didn't embarrass us. Our guests had also lost some—if not all—of their possessions. We were all in the same boat. In our new dining room, we shared hearty laughs with many of our displaced friends and neighbors.

The laughter wasn't coming just from our home. Across Lakeview, people were getting in better spirits, and by the following spring, our community was showing some signs of life again. Student enrollment at St. Dominic continued to rise. At Jesuit New Orleans, 1,285 of the original 1,450 students returned, including Chris. FEMA trailers dotted the area, providing temporary housing for residents committed to fixing up their properties.

Most of us were comparing notes about our individual issues and challenges. People frequently complained about a contractor or helper for this problem or that. At times, it reminded me of old people comparing their respective ailments, with all of them trying to "one up" each other about the seriousness of their respective problems. The one thing we could all agree on: It was a challenging year full of unexpected ups and downs and creative solutions for our community.

That May, LeBlanc reflected on the challenging school year in a touching letter she wrote for a Mass on the last day of school. She thanked the teachers, the staff, and the parents, and then she summed up the year perfectly in a few short phrases. "It was overwhelming," she said. "We suffered great losses and heartbreaking setbacks; but . . . we came to realize that the strength we need is within us."

NEW ORLEANS, LA. (Aug. 28, 2008) - Trumpeter Irvin Mayfield shows President George W. Bush the Elysian Trumpet during a dinner with cultural and community leaders at Dooky Chase Restaurant. Dedicated to those who perished in Hurricane Katrina, the trumpet is named for the neighborhood where Mr. Mayfield's father drowned during the storm. Representing New Orlean's spirit, the instrument is decorated with symbols of the city. White House photo by Chris Greenberg. Image courtesy of Wikimedia Commons.

NEW ORLEANS, LA. (Nov. 11, 2005) - On the Metarie side of the 17th Street Canal, a woman walks her dog along the levee beside the flood-wall. In the distance to the right, ongoing repairs on the breech on the New Orleans side of the levee can be seen. Photo by Infrogmation. Courtesy of Wikimedia Commons.

NEW ORLEANS, LA. (Sept. 14, 2005) - Large parts of New Orleans remain flooded two weeks after several levees failed in the wake of Hurricane Katrina. Bob McMillan/ FEMA Photo. Courtesy of Wikimedia Commons.

Airboats rescuing people in Lakeview. Photo courtesy of St. Dominic School, 2005.

NEW ORLEANS, LA. (Sept. 4, 2005) - A Texas Army National Guard Black Hawk deposits a 6,000 pound-plus bag of sand and gravel on-target as work progresses to close the breach in the 17th Street Canal. (U.S. Army Corp of Engineers photo by Alan Dooley). Courtesy of Wikimedia Commons.

Harrison Avenue in Lakeview is completely flooded. Photo courtesy of St. Dominic School, 2005.

St. Dominic Church in Lakeview. Photo courtesy of St. Dominic School, 2005.

A light pole leaning from Hurricane Katrina winds at the corner of Harrison Avenue and Vicksburg. St. Dominic sign is visible. Photo courtesy of St. Dominic, 2005.

The sign indicating the community of Lakeview. Photo courtesy of St. Dominic School, 2005.

Debris is piled high on West End Boulevard in Lakeview. Photo courtesy of St. Dominic School, 2005.

St. Dominic thanking Holy Rosary Academy for the temporary use of their campus. Photo courtesy of St. Dominic School, 2005.

NEW ORLEANS, LA. (April 20, 2006) - House in formerly flooded neighborhood of Eastern New Orleans has sign "Already Looted Twice." Photo by Infrogmation. Courtesy of Wikimedia Commons.

Sign celebrating the return of St. Dominic School in Lakeview. Photo courtesy of St. Dominic School, 2005.

New Orleans after Hurricane Katrina: House in formerly flooded Lakeview neighborhood with FEMA trailer and flag. Photo by Infrogmation. Courtesy of Wikimedia Commons.

Bill Herrington, Father Dan Lahart, and Chris Herrington. Photo by Rick Rivers of Strake Jesuit, 2016.

CHAPTER 11

STIRRING UP THE HORNETS

Wednesday, March 8, 2006
Months after the storm

On March 8, 2006, a near sell-out crowd gathered at what was then called the New Orleans Arena to watch the Hornets play the Los Angeles Lakers. The game signified more than basketball.

When the Hornets moved to New Orleans from Charlotte, North Carolina, four years earlier, many viewed the relocation as a sign of the city's corporate reinvigoration. Important companies for years had been leaving for a number of reasons, but now here was one who arrived to make New Orleans one of just a handful of American cities with two professional sports teams. And supporting the team was fun for my fellow New Orleanians and me as we cheered our Hornets to playoff appearances in two of their first three seasons after the move.

Then, Katrina happened. The Hornets played their fourth season in Oklahoma City while their hometown recovered, and the Saints, born in 1967, based themselves out of San Antonio. Many feared both the Hornets and the Saints would be added to the long list of things that the floodwaters swept away and would never give back. But the basketball team's first game in New Orleans after the storm was a reason to be optimistic that the city and its proud residents could rise from Katrina without having to give up everything that mattered to them.

That night, Frances and I were among 15,000 fans who were anxious to welcome their Hornets back and flocked to an arena still under repair. We wondered who would end up in the two club seats next to us, which were right behind the Hornets bench and in clear view of the television cameras. They had been owned by our friends Jud and Jeannie Grady, but they moved to Houston permanently after Katrina.

We also worried whether the team and the fans would be the same. So much had happened since we had last been together, and overall, it had been quite a journey to get to this night.

An Exhilarating Coup Before the storm

To tell the story of the Hornets in New Orleans, I have to tell the story of its owner, George Shinn. Born into a poor family in Kannapolis, North Carolina, Shinn's father died when he was eight, forcing his mother to work at several jobs just to keep him in hand-me-down clothes. He remembered being humiliated when a fifth grade classmate announced that Shinn was receiving free school lunches. He would later openly disclose that he graduated last in his high school class of 232 from A.L. Brown High School. Meanwhile, he worked in a variety of odd jobs, including a car wash and as a school janitor. His early life experiences made Shinn a driven man.

After high school, things changed for Shinn. He went on to Evans Business College in Concord, North Carolina, where he was influenced by Norman Vincent Peale's classic book, *The Power of Positive Thinking*. After graduating from Evans, Shinn raised some money and bought the

Evans Business College as well as some other small ones. He rolled all of the colleges up under the name of Rutledge Education Systems. Before selling his business, at one point Shinn had the largest chain of privately owned proprietary school systems in the country, including consulting contracts with more than 100 schools around the United States. In 1975, Shinn was inducted into the Horatio Alger Association. At the time, he was the youngest person ever to be presented with the Horatio Alger award. Shinn credits his mother with teaching him the "Triangle to Success," which he says is health, a positive attitude, and faith—faith both in God and in himself. In fact, faith is all that Shinn had to start with. He made himself from absolutely nothing.

With the proceeds of the sale of the business school, Shinn successfully bid on a new NBA franchise in 1987. The team would be named the Charlotte Hornets.

In 2002, the Hornets left Charlotte for New Orleans, in pursuit of a new stadium and better revenue-sharing arrangements. They were reluctantly given permission to move, only after exhaustive pleading to a skeptical NBA.

The move was a big deal to New Orleanians because they had lost a basketball team twenty-three years earlier, when the Jazz had abruptly left New Orleans for Salt Lake City in 1979. It was one of the least logical destinations for a team named "the Jazz." The owners of the Jazz, Sam Battistone and Larry Hatfield, had snatched the team from New Orleans like the Grinch who stole Christmas. At the time, the owners had complained about the lack of corporate support as well as an unfavorable lease arrangement. Nevertheless, it felt like theft, and egos in New Orleans had been badly bruised after the Jazz moved.

And times were changing in The Big Easy. A new cooperative spirit had emerged across the region to attempt to reverse the steady decline the area had experienced over the preceding decades. In fact, an Associated Press reporter described the years-long, multi-parish, public and private cooperative effort to return the National Basketball Association to the city of New Orleans as "unprecedented." The efforts were working. The NBA's Hornets had received conditional approval to move their franchise to New Orleans. Now, the last step to secure final consent for the relocation was the pre-sale of a minimum number of season tickets, suites, and corporate sponsorships. The AP news wire described the situation on January 18th of that year:

Hornets to move to New Orleans (Redacted)

MARY FOSTER, AP Sports Writer
Published Friday, January 18, 2002

NEW ORLEANS — An agreement to bring the Charlotte Hornets to New Orleans was announced Thursday by Louisiana Gov. Mike Foster, who said he was certain NBA owners will approve the move.

... The effort to sell tickets and suites would not be confined to just the city, Mayor Marc Morial said.

"We want you to know that the approach that we're taking is that this is going to be a team for southeast Louisiana, and for the entire state," Morial said.

At the conclusion of Morial's comments, spoken in the basketball arena, the Mayor quickly picked up a basketball, turned to the hoop, and launched a twenty-foot shot toward the goal. All eyeballs in the arena, at least a thousand, tracked the flight of the ball as it swished through the net. Morial did not hesitate with his shot. The gesture was meant to symbolize that New Orleans would do everything necessary to secure the relocation of the team. And the cocksure Morial had nailed it.

The announcement was an exhilarating coup for a city that desperately needed a corporate relocation victory. New Orleans had been declining economically since the 1980s, and few large corporations remained to buy the tickets and suites that the NBA required to approve relocation. But New Orleanians love their sports, and there was nothing better to bring the long suffering region together than to rally the community around returning pro basketball to the city.

Yet the move would be more than simply the return of professional basketball. New Orleans was tired of losing corporate headquarters and jobs. The relocation would send a statement to the rest of the country that New Orleans was open for business and that—in the name of commercial progress—the region was willing to finally put aside political corruption, infighting, and bickering among local parish leaders.

But a reputation for political corruption and incompetence preceded New Orleans, and both the NBA as well as its commissioner, David Stern, remained skeptical about whether the region had closed that chapter of its history. Well aware of Louisiana's political past, Stern was anxious about this move. Few could forget that Louisiana voters had propelled former Ku Klux Klan leader David Duke into a runoff election for governor only ten years before. Had the state really progressed that much in a decade, he wondered?

The Easiest $20 I Ever Made

With David Stern casting a wary eye toward New Orleans from his NBA headquarters perch on Fifth Avenue in New York, the Crescent City undertook the difficult task of securing the pre-sale of a minimum number of seats, suites, and corporate sponsorships. Two emerging private sector community leaders primarily led this effort.

One of the leaders was Doug Thornton. As a prep athlete in Shreveport, Thornton played under the enormous shadows cast by NFL stars Terry Bradshaw and Joe Ferguson, his predecessors as quarterback of the Woodlawn High School football team. But, as a grown-up, he had carved a name out for himself as the local chief of SMG, which holds the contract to oversee what is now known as the Mercedes-Benz Superdome. Further, since 1988, Thornton had successfully led New Orleans' effort to host a number of coveted sporting events—one of the few areas of economic success for the city—including Super Bowls, Final Fours, and others.

The other leader was Bill Hines, the managing partner of the Jones Walker law firm who was described in a March 2004 New Orleans *CityBusiness* article as a "speed talking corporate lawyer deluxe." The recipient of numerous civic awards and distinctions, including the Junior Achievement Hall of Fame award in 2012, Bill is an attorney who possesses an unrivaled passion for New Orleans civic involvement. As *The Times-Picayune* reported in 2013, "Hines sits on the boards of a staggering number of organizations, including the New Orleans Regional Medical Complex, the Greater New Orleans Sports Foundation, UNITY of Greater New Orleans, the New Orleans Recreation Department Foundation, and the Tulane University President's Council."

Almost everyone in the New Orleans area with a civic-minded bone in their body became involved in the effort to buy or sell something to secure the relocation of the Hornets. Volunteers were enlisted to man a phone bank at the New Orleans arena to call and encourage reluctant buyers. Organizers circulated lists of prominent business owners to the phone bank teams, and papers identified the best points of contact. The sale of basic tickets went reasonably well, but the more expensive sales of suites and sponsorships did not, as David Stern had worried. In fact, around March of 2002, not a single large corporate sponsorship had been sold, and the team desperately looked for an anchor sponsor to keep alive the dream of a Hornets move to New Orleans.

That was when Hibernia entered the scene, taking my personal interest in New Orleans' professional sports to an entirely new level. As the major bank in town and the official bank of the Saints, I knew it wouldn't be long before the Hornets came knocking on our door looking for our sponsorship. I was intrigued at the thought of Hibernia becoming the official bank of the Hornets, but I understood the challenges this would pose. We were already the sponsor of the Saints, and the sponsorship of both professional sports teams—the Saints and the Hornets—in New Orleans would at best be an expensive long shot.

However, no other notable corporate relocation to New Orleans had happened in the recent past. The Freeport-McMoRan relocation to New Orleans in the 1980s was the last major headquarters move, and this Hornets move was going to garner a lot of attention. I coveted the sponsorship and what it could mean for our banking franchise, and the thought of another bank seizing the role annoyed me.

I eventually explained the situation to our group head at Hibernia, Randy Howard. A man who was as comfortable with welders in a shipyard as in a corporate board room, Randy helped me convene an executive meeting to discuss the sponsorship. He was another Mississippi native and small community banker who had sold his bank to Hibernia. The combination of his self-deprecating style and self-described country-boy charm made him polished, charismatic, and full of a boatload of common sense.

The meeting, though, was a complete air ball, to borrow a basketball term. Hibernia CEO Herb Boydstun's sole focus was making the company more profitable, and he was appalled we would even suggest juggling two sports sponsorships that required an investment of millions of dollars over several years.

We nonetheless persisted in explaining the direct and indirect benefits of the sponsorship. And, as the meeting began to move to a close, Herb asked all of the participating managers how much they could contribute from their business lines in order to come up with the money. Most in attendance, including Kyle Waters, head of the retail bank, were proponents of the idea and pledged support for it. Only one executive declined. However, we were still $200,000 short of what was needed for the sponsorship, and I thought the idea would die.

Then, Herb surprised me. He closed the meeting by saying that he would erase the gap with $200,000 out of his CEO budget. Yet, as he expressed his commitment, he qualified his support by saying, "I'll agree to do this if it gets that far. But it won't. This team is not coming here, and this is a complete waste of time."

He then made a bet with me. I'd give him one dollar if the team didn't move to New Orleans. He'd give me twenty bucks if the team did move.

Though the meeting at one point had bruised my spirits, the pain didn't linger. Excitement at the thought of potentially becoming the first major sponsor to commit to the Hornets took over, and I accepted the bet.

Now, I wasn't entirely sure the Hornets were coming to New Orleans. But I was sure they were leaving Charlotte, North Carolina, because that community had refused a new arena for the Hornets and their primary owner, George Shinn. Also, at the time, there were only two NBA-ready arenas in the United States in cities that didn't have a franchise. One was in Louisville, Kentucky. The other was in New Orleans, where the wily Louisiana Gov. Edwin Edwards had pushed the construction of an NBA-caliber arena through the legislature in 1994—a building next door to the Superdome that would later end up flooded in Katrina. I figured I had a fifty-fifty chance to win, so I made the wager with Herb.

Later that day we called the Hornets' headquarters and committed to our sponsorship. The power company Entergy and beer distributor Southern Eagle, both clients of the bank, had contacted us earlier to see what we planned to do in support of the Hornets. After learning of Hibernia's commitment that afternoon, Entergy and Southern Eagle committed as sponsors the following day. A steady stream of sponsorships, commitments to lease suites, and promises to purchase tickets followed.

Then, on May 22, 2002, the Hornets received approval to move to New Orleans. As the late Mary Foster of the Associated Press wrote:

NEW ORLEANS — In the end, the vote that cleared the way for the Hornets to leave Charlotte was a Big Easy. NBA owners voted 28-1 Friday to approve the team's move at the conclusion of this season. Team owners George Shinn and Ray Wooldridge, reviled in Charlotte, paraded behind a brass band as they entered a news conference in their new city among a cadre of politicians.

The celebration came a little more than two hours after the NBA announced that representatives of the league's 29 ownership groups had voted to approve the Hornets' move from Charlotte. The move to Louisiana came after an unprecedented effort by city and state officials, members of Congress and civic leaders to convince NBA officials that the pover-

*ty-riddled state's economic future is bright and that
the financially struggling city could support a second
pro-sports franchise in addition to the NFL's Saints.*

*Business leaders spearheaded an effort to sell season
tickets and suites, eventually exceeding the league's
goals. When the Hornets gave their last update, they
had sold more than 10,500 season tickets and had
three-to-five-year agreements on 55 luxury suites. . . .*

Landing the Hornets was a resounding victory for
the region and for Metrovision, a super chamber of
commerce of which Bill Hines was president. As local
political commentator Clancy DuBos reported, "If anyone
ever doubted the mission and viability of Metrovision,
let them be silenced. The organization, which promotes
regional cooperation for economic development, scored
a three-pointer with the Hornets deal."

Hines and Doug Thornton were the toast of the town,
and they deserved it. Doug remained with SMG and
focused on the preparations to host the Hornets. Hines,
emboldened with the relocation success, became even more
energized on efforts pertaining to civic matters, and he
dedicated more of his time and energy to Metrovision.

For his part, George Shinn[11] had certainly made a name

---

[11] Interestingly, Shinn was a factor in placing three, or 10 percent, of
the NBA's 30 franchises in their current cities. First is the original
Hornets franchise, awarded to him in 1988 but then replaced by the
Bobcats in 2004. Charlotte's team is now again named the Hornets.
The second was the Thunder, formerly known as the Seattle Supersonics, who
moved to Oklahoma City after that community proved its ability to sustain a
franchise when it hosted the Hornets during their displacement after Katrina.
Of course, the third was New Orleans' NBA franchise, known today as the
Pelicans after Tom Benson purchased the team and changed its name from
the Hornets in 2012. Benson, also the Saints owner, would never have had the
opportunity to own an NBA team if Shinn had elected to sell New Orleans'
franchise to Oracle CEO Larry Ellison, who reportedly coveted the club a year
earlier and planned to move it to San Jose, California.

for himself. He emerged as a community leader and gave his time and money to the poor in the community. He had accomplished his goals of a new stadium and improved finances in the first three years the team was in New Orleans prior to Katrina. And many fans supported both the Hornets and the Saints, even seeking the Hornets out as an alternative to the Saints. Some who were primarily dedicated to the Saints killed time in between seasons by pulling for the Hornets.

Following all of the excitement of the Hornets' announcement, the first executive meeting was held at Hibernia. There was a metaphorical elephant in the room at that gathering: the bet I had made with Herb. However, I knew better than to mention it and tread on his nerves again. Finally, at the end of the meeting, Kyle Waters said, "Herb, I think you owe Bill some money, don't you?"

Herb grumbled for a moment, but in the end he reached into his back pocket for his wallet. Begrudgingly, he pulled out a $20 bill.

I've often wondered what would have happened if Herb had not stepped up for the extra $200,000 that day. I've been thankful that he did—as the rest of New Orleans basketball fans should be. Perhaps another Hornets anchor sponsor would have committed if we had not. We will never know.

And in the study at my home, a $20 bill and an announcement of the Hornets' relocation are proudly framed and displayed on the wall, proof of the big gamble that had paid off.

Unfortunately, a few years later, that prized $20 bill would be hanging in a room that was flooded by Hurricane Katrina, with mold creeping up the walls toward it. It seemed to be framed in a sea of hopelessness, along with the improvements throughout the city that were trapped in the flood as well.

An Unforgettable Return

But after the storm, businesses and residents slowly returned to New Orleans. From January 2006 through that spring, things were gradually getting back to normal in the city. Soon, with New Orleans in full renovation mode, all eyes began to turn toward accomplishing two of the more important priorities for many in the community: bringing back the NFL's Saints and NBA's Hornets. After the storm, the Hornets had temporarily relocated to Oklahoma City, and the Saints had relocated to San Antonio.

Doug Thornton, the SMG executive who had spearheaded the Hornets' relocation in 2002, would have to get to work again to helping repair both the Superdome and the New Orleans Arena so that both teams could again have home venues. But instead of asking a fragile market to support two professional teams in 2006, Thornton recommended to the governor that the Hornets play both the 2005-06 and the 2006-07 NBA seasons in Oklahoma City. As he told *The Times-Picayune*, he recalled thinking, "Let's give the market a chance to recover."

From a practical standpoint, Thornton absolutely made the right call. The city needed time to heal, and Thornton needed time to put his arenas back together again.

The primary focus was on the Saints. After all, the team had been born in New Orleans, when the NFL had awarded the city and inaugural owner John Mecom the franchise on All Saints' Day in 1967. And New Orleans had supported the Saints since their infancy, even though it meant rooting for a losing team more often than not, such as the 1-15 "Aints" from 1980. Playoff victories, and even a Super Bowl championship, came after local New Orleanian Tom Benson purchased the team in 1985. Nonetheless, the truth is that loving the Saints through even the toughest of times was encoded into the DNA of every true New

Orleanian, and the thought of them ever playing anywhere else was simply . . . well, unthinkable.

In consultation with key NFL personnel, including then-Commissioner Paul Tagliabue and current Commissioner Roger Goodell, officials developed a plan to get the Superdome operational by January 2007. But soon thereafter, Goodell called Thornton. He wanted to know if there was any way Thornton could get the Dome open by September 2006—the NFL wasn't keen on the idea that the Saints would have to play two seasons away from New Orleans.

So Thornton gathered his staff and brought in architects to study plans that could ready the Superdome for the Saints in time for the 2006 NFL season. "I called Roger back and said, 'I think we can do it, but here are the conditions. We may not have all restrooms functional,'" Thornton said. "We may not have all the (luxury) suites finished. And we certainly won't have the (ritzy) club level done."

Goodell was fine with that. As long as the stadium was safe for fans, there was turf to play on, and the scoreboard worked, the Saints could come home. But first, Thornton had to convince Louisiana Governor Kathleen Blanco to issue an executive order empowering him and his staff to make decisions unilaterally and expedite the rebuilding effort at the Superdome. Blanco obliged.

Thornton began the challenging work of repairing two of the largest buildings in the state of Louisiana. He could zero his focus in on such a monumental task because of his wife, Denise. Denise Thornton contended with repairing her and her husband's home. It had taken on about ten feet of floodwater because it was near Lakeview and the breached levee along the 17th Street canal. She set up a "command center" of sorts at her home to help other neighbors with the myriad insurance and construction issues as well as other red tape folks had to navigate to rebuild. And she pushed New Orleans' power, sewerage, trash and cable companies to restore basic services to her neighborhood sooner than they probably otherwise would have.[12]

The decision to stagger the return of the sports teams appears to have been a wise choice, and the Thornton's tireless efforts paid off for their beloved city. The Saints returned home for a memorable victory over the Atlanta Falcons on September 25, 2006, on "Monday Night Football." That game produced an unforgettable play by special-teams ace Steve Gleason[13], who blocked a punt that resulted in a first-quarter touchdown for the home team. It was a night that no one in New Orleans will ever forget.

While the Saints experienced a successful return, things were a bit more complicated with the Hornets. The hard truth was that the Hornets were a relative newcomer to the city, and their owner, George Shinn, did not grow up in the city like the Saints' owner, Tom Benson, had. Although we'd rolled out the red carpet for them, people still worried whether George Shinn and the Hornets would return.

From a financial perspective, the storm could not have come along at a worse time for Shinn. George had taken on a lot of debt prior to the 2005-2006 season to buy out his minority partner, Ray Wooldridge. The financial stress after the storm would be enormous for Shinn. His mother's teachings about faith and a positive attitude would be even more critical than ever in this fourth season in New Orleans.

---

[12] Denise Thornton's efforts inspired her to establish the Beacon of Hope Resource Center. With 25 satellite offices and 30,000 volunteers, the resource center assisted more than 31,000 households affected by Katrina, playing a key factor in repopulating and redeveloping New Orleans' neighborhoods following the storm, according to the group's website.

[13] Gleason is now a highly-respected advocate for people who, like him, suffer from amyotrophic lateral sclerosis, the neuromuscular disease commonly called "ALS" or "Lou Gehrig's disease."

At times, people have remarked to me that owning a sports franchise has got to be the easiest thing in the world and a certain path to astounding wealth. That perspective has surprised me. It's a business that is enormously complex and far from easy, especially in the NBA, where the league is structured with multi-year guaranteed contracts. And some fans want the owners to spend the maximum amount of money on players to get more wins, no matter the impact on the bottom line.

An owner has to deal with fans, sponsors, players' unions, sports agents, politicians, lenders and a thousand other things—all under an intense media spotlight. Owners have to watch every word they say and every action they take. It's a tough business. In fact, it may be one of the more difficult businesses to run—that is, if you want to make a profit and contend for championships.

Shinn needed to make a lot of income in order to service the debt he had taken out. To see his fan base evacuated and destitute was a most unwelcome surprise.

When Katrina struck, the Hornets had started practicing, and the first preseason game was less than a month away. Immediately after the storm, Shinn conferred with the NBA commissioner's office to develop a backup plan. On September 21, 2005, it was announced that the Ford Center in Oklahoma City would become the temporary home of the New Orleans Hornets.

But another thing changed, something that would cause anxiety among the team's fans in New Orleans. The team would be named the "New Orleans/Oklahoma City Hornets" as part of the "temporary" arrangement. Not only that, but fan attendance was noticeably different between the two cities at the time.

The Ford Center hosted thirty-six games in the 2005-06 season, one more than planned. Two games had been planned in Baton Rouge to stay in closer touch with the Louisiana fans. However, in the first game played on December 16th, 2005, only 7,302 fans attended a contest against Phoenix in the Pete Maravich Assembly Center on LSU's campus. The second planned game was canceled and moved back to Oklahoma City.

When the Ford Center wasn't available for a January 13, 2006 game, it was instead played at the University of Oklahoma in Norman. There, a whopping 11,343 fans watched the Hornets beat the Sacramento Kings in an 11,528-seat arena. Even the preseason crowds in Oklahoma City rivaled regular-season attendance in New Orleans. Fan attendance was 14,475 on October 23rd and 15,063 on October 27th.

The NBA noticed. Who would have thought that Oklahoma City would be such a good NBA market? But it was. Of the thirty-six games that Oklahoma City hosted, average attendance in the 19,163-seat Ford Center was 18,718, with more than half of the games being sellouts. They were eleventh in attendance in the NBA. Even though the team had a losing record overall and didn't make the playoffs, the team's record was 22-14 in the Ford Center. The fan base was going crazy in the Ford Center and was clearly making a difference in the win column.

All of this fan frenzy in Oklahoma was getting the Louisiana fan base really nervous, and the memories of losing the Jazz in 1979 recurred. Watching a team that had "Oklahoma City" as half of its name was making everyone in New Orleans uneasy, prompting some to say that the Hornets would never return.

But the Hornets belonged to New Orleans. And the people of Oklahoma City knew it. Oklahoma had dealt with their own horrible tragedy in April of 1995, when Timothy McVeigh bombed the Alfred P. Murrah Federal Building, killing 168 and injuring more than six hundred others. Oklahoma was sensitive to not taking advantage of New Orleans in a time of weakness. People there simply wanted to show the NBA and the world that their community was worthy of a team. They succeeded, and in 2008 they got their reward: their very own team, the Thunder. Shinn also promised to return to New Orleans. In an interview with ESPN on November 7, 2005, Shinn said, "People in New Orleans accepted us in a positive way (on the move from Charlotte), and I have to return the favor. We're going to do our part to make that city come back."

As he spoke those words, work had been steadily progressing at the New Orleans Arena. It was enough progress that Thornton was ready to commit to play three games in the arena in the midst of renovation.

Shinn kept his promise when the Hornets showed up to the arena to play the L.A. Lakers on March 8, 2006.

"Awn it Like a Hawnet"

Frances and I arrived at the New Orleans arena that night with anticipation. As the banker of the Hornets, I was a big Hornets fan, as was Frances. We waited eagerly for the return of the team and our friends, George Shinn and his wife, Denise. George was a practical joker and a bit of a rascal who nicknamed Denise, an attractive former nurse, "Nurse Goodbody." We also eyed the empty seats next to us, wondering who would sit there.

When our new neighbors finally found their seats next to us at the game, we introduced ourselves. They turned out to be huge Hornets fans and loud and proud residents of what they called "St. Bernawd Parish." They were speaking in "full yat" dialect, the most pronounced version of a New Orleans accent.

"Yat" is a term derived from the local greeting, "Where y'at?" Natives often speak with varying degrees of the

Brooklyn-esque accent, ranging from just a bit of Yat to what is considered "full Yat," depending on geographic and social factors. The type, strength, and delivery of the accent vary from section to section of the New Orleans metro area, marking distinctions between income, ethnicities, and neighborhoods. That's why, when I've been asked what a New Orleans accent sounds like, I always reply, "Well, it depends on where you're from in the city."

Locals take pride in the various distinctive speech patterns, which are as diverse as the history of the city itself, and longtime residents can often tell what area other locals are from by their accent. A. J. Liebling's book, *The Earl of Louisiana,* details the origins of the accents in a passage used as a foreword to *A Confederacy of Dunces,* John Kennedy Toole's famous, posthumously published novel set in New Orleans:

"There is a New Orleans city accent . . . associated with downtown New Orleans, particularly with the German and Irish Third Ward, that is hard to distinguish from the accent of Hoboken, Jersey City, and Astoria, Long Island, where the Al Smith inflection, extinct in Manhattan, has taken refuge. The reason, as you might expect, is that the same stocks that brought the accent to Manhattan imposed it on New Orleans."

Perhaps the reason our new seat neighbors from St. Bernard had such a distinctive "full yat" accent could be traced back to 1927. Although the working-class community of St. Bernard had dealt with many natural disasters, the Mississippi River flood of 1927 was perhaps its biggest.

That year, the river had risen so high that it had threatened the heart of the city of New Orleans. In order to protect New Orleans, the city elders blew the levee downriver from New Orleans, flooding St. Bernard and devastating most of the parish. The people of St. Bernard developed a well-founded distrust of New Orleanians after the 1927 flood and perhaps wanted to sound nothing like them. The parish rebuilt, but it learned to rely on their St. Bernard neighbors—not the elite New Orleanians who had flooded them out.

Whatever the reason, our neighbors certainly spoke "full yat." They dropped endings such as –er and –ing off words, pronouncing *player* and *playing* as *playuh* and *playin*. They also pronounced vowels as "ah" or "aw," so *heart, God,* and *New Orleans* sounded like *hawt, Gawd,* and *New Awlens.*

Their phrase of the night was "awn it like a Hawnet," which they repeated over and over. My new friend loved the phrase so much that he made a sign that folded out to read, "On it like a Hornet." The sign was probably ten feet long, and he insisted that everyone in our row participate in holding up the sign to ensure exposure on television.

"I love dat phrase, man. Don't ya love it?" he asked enthusiastically.

I thought about telling him his phrase might not resonate as well to those outside of St. Bernard Parish, but I thought better of it. For one, it was the first night back for the "Hawnets," and I didn't want to be called a "pawty poopah."

Plus, every authentic New Orleanian speaks at least a little yat. I can say this with confidence because every New Orleanian is either a Saints fan or has at least been to a game. (If they haven't seen or been to one, I don't think they can claim to be a bona fide New Orleanian.) At every Saints game the familiar chant is heard, "Who dat say dey gonna beat dem Saints? Who dat, who dat!" And if the Saints win, the excitement takes over and even the most proper linguists can transform from "lite yat" to medium or even full yat for the rest of the day. On Mondays after a Saints win, two simple words are all that need to be said to celebrate civic pride and a New Orleans victory. "Who dat!"

That first night back at the arena, it was rockin', and our entire row got in the spirit, yelling "awn it like a Hawnet" the rest of the night. It was a great "pawty," as my seat neighbor called it. He loved the phrase so much he was going to get it "patented," he said. We—including George Shinn and his beloved "Nurse Goodbody"—had a lot of fun.

It was a great night to be back in New Orleans.

Reflecting back on the significance of sports that year, Doug Thornton said in interview with *The Times-Picayune*, "I don't want to overstate this, but what if we had failed? What if we had not been able to (be) successful? What if the Saints couldn't have come back? What if the Hornets hadn't come back? Would New Orleans be the place it is today?"

I don't believe New Orleans would be in the place it is today without the return of the Saints and the Hornets and all of the people who made their return possible. Not only did New Orleanians triumph in getting their teams back, but the victories would keep coming on the court and on the field as the city continued to recover from the storm. The Hornets would have the most successful season in franchise history when they returned to New Orleans full-time for the 2007-08 campaign, making it to Game 7 of the Western Conference semifinals before being eliminated. And fewer than four years after returning to the Superdome, the Saints would win their first—and, as of 2016, only—Super Bowl title, in Miami on Feb. 7, 2010.

Photograph of the renovated New Orleans superdome, home of the New Orleans Saints, and New Orleans arena, home of the New Orleans Hornets (now named the New Orleans Pelicans). Photo by Wikimedia Commons.

CHAPTER 12

VISITING MR. HARRIGAN

Saturday, May 20, 2006
Eight months after the storm

As Frances and I continued to renovate our house until it was fully repaired, we received some unanticipated news. My job changed, and my company asked me to move back permanently to Houston. Just like that, Frances and I were preparing for yet another move to Houston.

We spent weeks bidding farewell to our friends in New Orleans. On our last afternoon in New Orleans, I had one last loose end I wanted to tie up before the movers arrived the following morning. I had never learned what happened to Mr. Harrigan after we had rescued him from being stranded at his home shortly after the storm and had watched him fly off in the Coast Guard helicopter. So I told Katherine, who was with me, that we were going to see someone.

"Sure," Katherine said, "but who is it?" I understood the question. We had already said goodbye to what seemed like a million people.

I asked her if she remembered when I told her about "putting the man in the helicopter." She said she did.

"Well, I'd like to run by to see what happened to him," I told her. She hopped in the car with me, and we drove together toward Mr. Harrigan's street.

The Four-Letter Word

We passed houses in varying states of reconstruction. Some houses sat unrepaired, their homeowners still negotiating with their insurance companies and bogged down with endless red tape and disputes.

Katherine and I continued on, past trailers that were parked on homeowners' properties or in their driveways, the only habitable dwelling option for residents who didn't have an upstairs like us. The trailers had been issued by FEMA, which was an acronym for The Federal Emergency Management Agency of the United States Department of Homeland Security. Its mission was to coordinate the response to disasters that overwhelm the resources of local and state authorities.

Unfortunately, local residents experienced more bureaucratic delays in the aftermath of the storm than relief from FEMA. The acronym for the agency was so reviled that the people of New Orleans came to regard it in the same manner they do other bad four-letter words.

As we neared Mr. Harrigan's home, I swerved to avoid a huge pothole. I had to be especially alert to prevent the numerous potholes plaguing the streets. The streets that had once been well-paved were now threatening to wreck the bottom of my car.

As it turned out, the pumps designed back in the early 1900s to protect the area from flooding may have been too efficient. By removing water from the city as fast and as efficiently as possible, the underlying spongy delta soil in and around New Orleans was deprived of the natural saturation it needed to remain stable.

Later, the fear of flooding and the obsession with removing floodwater quickly would evolve to also include the issue of soil subsidence. A grassroots effort to confront the problem saw Lakeview homeowners placing signs in their front yards pleading, "Fix our streets." The so-called Greater New Orleans Water Plan would emerge to help address these subsidence concerns.

But before all that, in my car with Katherine, I continued on, turned a corner, and there it was. Mr. Harrigan's home.

Mr. Harrigan

I pulled my car to a stop in front of his house. I noticed a FEMA trailer was installed on his front lawn.

I had tried to suppress my memories of when I met him that day nine months earlier. But as I got out of the car and looked around, the memories rumbled back. I couldn't believe the street had been flooded with five feet of water less than a year ago. Now, the yard had been cleared of debris, but there was no vegetation beyond a few clumps of weeds. The brackish floodwater had killed all other landscaping that had once been there.

As we approached the trailer, Katherine asked anxiously, "Is anybody in there, Dad? Is it okay for us to be here?" She sounded nervous.

"It's fine," I told her. "We should see if Mr. Harrigan is in the trailer."

I knocked on the door. Nothing. So I waited a bit and knocked again.

"Who is it?" I heard from inside.

The tone of the voice I heard and the situation in general seemed strangely similar to our first encounter.

"Mr. Harrigan, it's your neighbor," I said. "Just coming by to check on you."

Mr. Harrigan replied, "Okay, give me a minute."

The door eventually opened about six inches, just enough so Mr. Harrigan could get a good look at me from inside.

"Mr. Harrigan, I'm Bill Herrington from the flood," I said. "Do you remember me?"

He didn't. I felt a twinge of sadness.

"We came in the boat and put you in the helicopter," I said, hoping to jog his memory.

"Well, I remember a girl," he said. I assumed he meant Frances, who was with me the day we loaded him into the Coast Guard helicopter. Mr. Harrigan looked over at my anxious daughter. "Is that her?" he asked.

"No, this is my daughter, Katherine," I explained. "The girl you remember was my wife, Frances." Frances had comforted Mr. Harrigan and held his hand on the boat ride. After I mentioned Frances' name and introduced him to Katherine, his apprehension vanished, and he invited us in.

As he cleared space for us to sit, I looked around his small trailer. A few things salvaged from the flood lay on a bench inside, mostly framed photographs of his family. One that struck me was of what looked like a much younger, fitter, and trimmer version of Mr. Harrigan, neatly dressed in a military uniform.

"Is this you, Mr. Harrigan?" I asked, trying to make small talk.

"Yes," he said. "That's me from the war."

I admired that what he displayed most prominently in his trailer after all we had been through were his family photographs. Many people realize what's most important to them after being affected by natural disasters. I counted myself as one, and it seemed I was in good company with Mr. Harrigan.

"Mr. Harrigan, what happened to you after we put you in the helicopter?" I asked.

It soon became clear that Mr. Harrigan had plenty to tell. It seemed he had been cooped up in his trailer by himself for many months and that few had been there to listen until Katherine and I arrived.

Mr. Harrigan recounted how the helicopter crew took him to Barksdale Air Force Base in Shreveport, Louisiana, about three hundred miles northwest of New Orleans. There, Mr. Harrigan said, U.S. Secretary of Defense Donald Rumsfeld greeted him.

"I guess someone had told him I was coming because he seemed to know," Mr. Harrigan said. "He took a special interest in me and made sure they took good care of me."

After staying there for a bit, Mr. Harrigan said, the base sent him up north to be with his son.

"You know, if you listen to the news, you would think that no one from the Bush administration was anywhere near us during Katrina," Mr. Harrigan said. "But Rumsfeld was right there, I assure you." He emphasized the last part about Rumsfeld being there.

I agreed with Mr. Harrigan. The media had mostly focused on the trapped families—predominantly African-American—at the Superdome and the convention center. But this storm had indiscriminately wiped out nearly everything in its path. Rich, poor, black and white—nearly everyone and everything was affected.

The heart of uptown New Orleans had not been too drastically damaged, but the suburbs of Lakeview and Old Metairie had been badly flooded, affecting a significant number of upper- and middle-class families, black and white. And Lakeview, Metairie and Uptown New Orleans had similar populations. The media covered less of this. Either they didn't know or chose to not report that Rumsfeld had been at the base Mr. Harrigan was taken to in Shreveport during rescue efforts. I later remember how surprised some folks outside of Louisiana were when they learned our home in Metairie had flooded. That was how influential the selection of new stories by the media was.

Mr. Harrigan and I exchanged post-storm stories for another ten minutes or so while Katherine listened quietly but intently. I wondered if she had picked up on the political significance of the Rumsfeld anecdote.

We asked Mr. Harrigan if he needed anything, but he assured us he was fine. Someone had been bringing him hot meals, he said, and we believed him when he mentioned being content.

As we stood up to leave, I shook Mr. Harrigan's hand. My daughter gave him a hug. We then said one last goodbye.

Looking Back

On our way back to the car, I stopped and looked around one last time. Life had partially returned to our neighborhood by that May of 2006. A number of families we knew were now living in FEMA trailers or in their upstairs. Kids down the street played basketball. The birds chirped and a squirrel jumped across the branch of a tree that had survived the devastation. I remembered the tree from nine months earlier while I was aboard a flatboat navigating flooded streets.

The familiar sights and sounds encouraged me that things were getting better. But a few of the tree's limbs were crooked and twisted, reminding me of a badly broken arm that hadn't healed perfectly. It was getting better, but it would likely bear a permanent scar, like many of the people who had endured the storm.

Looking back, though, I realized that my loved ones and I got through it because of the wonderful folks we encountered. I imagine my family wasn't the only one who felt that way. From first responders to Jesuit teachers and priests to compassionate Houstonians, we had witnessed some of the best in people. We encountered people who opened their homes, schools, cities, and hearts to others in need. These people who aided their neighbors deserve a special place in heaven.

Sure, we also witnessed some of the worst in people—the looters, dishonest contractors, and others who preyed on people who were down and out just because they knew they could. But now, ten years later, I can honestly say that even the looters and the crooks were part of the reason why my family and many others emerged from the aftermath of the storm as stronger people.

And on the way to becoming stronger, we developed a bond that won't ever be broken.

No matter what storms lay ahead.

TEN YEARS AFTER THE STORM

It's hard to quantify how traumatic Hurricane Katrina was for New Orleanians and even those who tried to help them in their hour of need. For one, we may never know how many people the storm killed. According to the most credible source I found in my research, the storm killed at least 1,429 people in seven states. Of those deaths, 1,170 were Louisiana residents and another 259 deaths occurred in other states. However, if "indeterminate" death classifications are counted, the death toll could have been much higher.[14]

The data show that the Louisiana victims included men and women of all races. While most of those who died were black (53 percent), a significant number were white (38 percent). Others were reported as Hispanic, Asian, American Indian, and "other."

On another front, those in Houston who hosted evacuees after Katrina struggled to preserve the compassion and patience with which they initially confronted the situation. Even today, Houston's response to Katrina is controversial. Research conducted at Rice University's Kinder Institute for Urban Research by Dr. Stephen Klineberg showed that, by 2006, many Houstonians believed that helping those displaced by Katrina put a considerable strain on their community.[15] Almost half of those surveyed opined

---

[14] Maxwell, Poppy and Ratard, Raoult. "Deaths Directly Caused by Hurricane Katrina." Department of Health and Hospitals, State of Louisiana, 2014: http://new.dhh.louisiana.gov/assets/oph/Center-PHCH/Center-CH/stepi/specialstudies/KatrinaDeath1.pdf.

[15] Much of the data in this section is derived from the research of Stephen Klineberg, "Four Myths About Katrina's Impact on Houston." Urban Edge, Kinder Institute, August 26, 2015: http://urbanedge.blogs.rice.edu/2015/08/26/four-myths-about-katrinas-impact-on-houston/#.VwrLpzP2ZD9.

that the evacuees' impact on the Texas city was overall a bad thing, and as time went on, Dr. Klineberg's research showed that even more people agreed with those sentiments. Yet Klineberg's research wasn't all bad news. Not even a disaster like Katrina could drown out all of the good it took to overcome the storm, and his research unearthed an encouraging silver lining that justifies the faith people have in humanity.

Dr. Klineberg's research revealed that Houstonians surveyed in 2008 would likely help evacuees again, despite the negative feelings they expressed about the Katrina situation. Those surveyed were asked whether—if a storm like Katrina happened again—the Houston community should respond with more, less, or the same amount of assistance as in 2005. Fewer than three out of every ten people surveyed said Houston should respond with less assistance. Almost half called for the same level of response, and one out of every four people surveyed said the community should do even more. Houstonians demonstrated that they knew helping fellow Americans was the right thing to do, and for the most part they were willing to do it again.

Further, other data gathered by Dr. Klineberg quantified just how many Houstonians jumped to Katrina victims' aide immediately after the storm. Eighty-five percent of the people surveyed said they had either volunteered time or donated items such as money, food, and clothes to relief efforts. That amazing response isn't always the case, as Klineberg's research showed that levels of "community connectedness" in Houston are generally quite low, but Katrina brought that city together as never before, to the benefit of people in dire need.

As Dr. Klineberg wrote in a September 2015 article, "We don't know what this will mean for Houston in the long run, but the remarkable experience ten years ago of an entire urban community coming together to help people in need seems likely to have a lasting positive impact." As an off-again, on-again Houston resident since 1983, I would agree. In fact, I think it was Houston's finest hour, the one moment in time that best highlighted the true spirit and core values of Houstonians.

All of which brings me to the message I want this book to leave.

Disaster can strike at any time, and lives can be reversed on a dime, much like the sudden reversal of traffic we experienced in contraflow. Even families with resources and civic connections, like mine, experienced extreme difficulties in the aftermath of Katrina. However, the less fortunate members of a community will suffer the greatest impact of a disaster, particularly the children of these families who are at risk of falling through society's cracks. Children develop significant emotional and educational needs after disasters. Alice Graham Baker understood this when she and her friends established the predecessor of Neighborhood Centers, Inc. in 1907.

Calamity can—no, it *will*—test people's core values. These core values, if not abandoned, allow people to lead in times of crisis, as Judge Eckels and former Mayor White so capably demonstrated. And doing the right thing, even when it is challenging, is a test of humanity, as Father Lahart reminded me. These acts of kindness can have a lasting, positive impact on a community, as Dr. Klineberg suggested. And it is important to pay tribute to these acts whenever they occur.

Many New Orleanians have recovered well since the storm. Others may never fully recover. But all of them are people who were willingly living in an area vulnerable to storms, though also unknowingly living in an area with inferior and defective federal levees.

Thankfully, after more than a decade, officials have reportedly corrected and improved most of the levee systems. At least two historical markers have been erected at the 17th Street and London Avenue canals to remind future generations of how vital the integrity of the levees that protect New Orleans is.

I'll never forget how steep the cost of inferior levees can be. But I'll also never forget how, when those levees failed, countless people who helped those in need did not fail.

And I'll forever be thankful I got to meet some of them. In the course of telling this story, I introduced you to a lot of men and women. Here's what's become of them since our paths crossed:

Jim Meza: After leaving the University of New Orleans and New Beginnings in 2011, Meza became the superintendent of the Jefferson Parish Public School System. He retired from that position in 2014 and was then inducted into the Loyola University New Orleans Athletics Hall of Fame for his achievements while playing college baseball in the 1960s.

Kathleen Blanco: By early 2007, Blanco faced increasingly heated accusations of delays in administering a program that she and the Louisiana Recovery Authority had established following Katrina to distribute federal aid money to storm victims for damage to their homes. That January, not even two hundred fifty of about 100,000 "Road Home" program applicants had received money from the program, and many payments were based on erroneous assessments of damage to homes. As re-election time drew near and her popularity plummeted, Blanco deflected blame toward President Bush's administration. One notable instance was when Bush didn't mention the Gulf Coast's reconstruction efforts in his 2007 State of the Union Address, and Blanco asked Congress to probe whether partisan politics influenced the presidential administration's response following

Katrina. She also insinuated that Mississippi benefited from preferential treatment after Katrina because its governor at the time, Haley Barbour, is Republican. She ultimately announced that she would not seek re-election, and Republican Bobby Jindal succeeded her as governor.

Mary Landrieu: Landrieu won re-election to a third term in 2008, but a fourth term in the U.S. Senate was not in the cards for her. She was defeated in a runoff against Republican Bill Cassidy in December 2014. Landrieu stayed out of the public eye briefly but then emerged to rally support for Hillary Clinton's U.S. presidential campaign in 2016.

Ray Nagin: Nagin served as New Orleans' mayor until 2010, when he was succeeded by Senator Landrieu's brother, Mitch. In 2014, Nagin was sentenced to 10 years in federal prison on charges that he accepted bribes by people courting business from the city when he was mayor. Nagin is the lone New Orleans mayor to ever be indicted on or convicted of corruption charges.

Edwin Edwards: In 2002, around the time the New Orleans Hornets began playing in an arena he advocated building, Edwin Edwards began serving a federal prison sentence on corruption charges stemming from a scheme involving riverboat casino licenses. He was released in 2011 and three years later unsuccessfully ran for a U.S. Congressional seat.

Sherriff Newell Normand: The political protégé of longtime Jefferson Parish Sheriff Harry Lee, who died in October 2007, Normand was elected to his first term as sheriff a month later by more than 90 percent of voters who cast ballots. He won re-election with similar ease in 2011 and 2015.

Retired U.S. Army Lt. General Russel L. Honoré: The commander of Joint Task Force Katrina who coordinated post-hurricane relief efforts in New Orleans in 2005 retired in 2008. He is now an environmental activist who dedicates his life to helping communities better prepare themselves to withstand natural disasters. Honoré also leads The Honoré Center for Undergraduate Student Achievement in New Orleans, Louisiana.

Steve Hebert: The man who remained in charge at the Hibernia Center even as it took on water during Katrina lives in Metairie with his wife of almost four decades, Judie. They have two daughters and two grandchildren, and they are expecting the arrival of a third grandchild in June 2016. In 2008, Hebert and his business partner, Blaine Gahagan, founded HGI, a full-service facility management and commercial real estate sales company. With twenty-seven employees and nine commercial real estate agents, they serve an area ranging from Texas to Florida and as far north as Arkansas.

Elliott J. "E.J." Raley III: E.J. Raley continues to work as an insurance agent, based out of the West Bank community of Harvey. He and his wife, Jan, live in Terrytown.

Herb Boydstun: Herb retired from the bank in 2006 and now lives in Baton Rouge with his wife, Nan.

Randall E. "Randy" Howard: The former Hibernia board member who helped convene an executive meeting to discuss Hibernia's possible sponsorship of the Hornets before the team moved from Charlotte to New Orleans is semi-retired. He lives in Thibodaux, Louisiana, and Jackson, Mississippi, with his wife, Carolyne. A proud father of two and grandfather of four, he is serving on the board of a bank in New Orleans and is the vice chairman of the board of a Mississippi bank.

George Shinn: George Shinn sold the New Orleans Hornets to the NBA in December 2010 and lives in Tennessee. Some writings on Shinn assert that he has since retired there, but he vehemently assured me that is not the case, saying that his final chapter is "to give money away to serve the Lord." He runs The George Shinn Foundation. The website, GeorgeShinnFoundation.org, documents the group's efforts and offers grants to initiatives that it considers worthy and that are in need of charitable funding. Meanwhile, the Hornets were sold by the NBA to the Saints' owner, Tom Benson, in 2012 and renamed the New Orleans Pelicans in time for their 2013-14 campaign.

Bill Goldring: Bill continues to own and run the Sazerac Company and the Buffalo Trace distillery. Sazerac occupied the last page of the July 2014 issue of Forbes magazine, along with its new bourbon brand, Fireball, which is popular both in New Orleans barrooms and along its parade routes. The Sazerac Company expanded further in 2016 with the acquisition of the Southern Comfort brand from Brown-Forman.

Robert Eckels: Robert Eckels remained a judge in Houston until 2007, when he left to practice law in the private sector. He and his colleagues have been on a mission to establish a bullet train line by 2021 that would take passengers from Dallas to Houston and vice versa in 90 minutes.

Bill White: Bill White remained Houston's mayor until early 2010. Months later, he unsuccessfully tried to unseat incumbent Texas Gov. Rick Perry. He was appointed chairman of the financial advisory and asset management firm Lazard Houston in 2012, and two years later he wrote a well-received book about the United States' growing federal debt crisis, *America's Fiscal Constitution*.

Mark Sloan: Mark received many awards and distinctions for his coordination under Judge Eckels of 60,000 volunteers following Hurricane Katrina, including ABC Nightly News' Person of the Week (2005) and "The President's Call to Service Award" (2007). Today he is the Homeland Security & Emergency Management Coordinator for Harris County as well as the director of Harris County Citizen Corps, an innovative, award-winning public preparedness initiative, recognized as a National Best Practice. He developed one of the first websites devoted to the sharing of community preparedness volunteer opportunities throughout the country at www.harriscountycitizencorps.com.

Bill Hines: Despite his role as managing partner at the powerful Jones Walker law firm in New Orleans, Bill Hines' involvement with civic associations has not waned over the years. He is chairman of an organization committed to ending homelessness in the area, and late in 2015 he received a "Distinguished Citizen" award from the Boy Scouts of America's Southeast Louisiana Council. He also reigned as Rex—or king of Carnival—on Fat Tuesday in 2013.

Father Flavio Bravo: After thirteen years at Strake Jesuit, Father Bravo accepted an assignment to become the superior at Compañia de Jesús of Puerto Rico in August 2015.

Father Daniel Lahart: Lahart served as president of Strake Jesuit from 2001 to 2016, a time during which he signed the diplomas of more than 3,000 of the nearly 8,000 Strake Jesuit graduates. In 2016, he stepped down from that position to become the president at Regis High School in New York City. Strake Jesuit's board of directors selected Father Jeff Johnson as Lahart's successor. Johnson was the assistant student affairs principal and taught English before being chosen for his new role. He has big shoes to fill, but right off the bat, it is clear from his words that he has the right attitude to thrive during the adventure ahead. Vowing to continue helping the school make "a lasting impact in the lives of many men throughout the Houston area," Johnson said after his promotion, "I'm very excited to ensure that our school will continue to lead the way in the formation and education of men for others."

Father Anthony McGinn: Jesuit New Orleans' president when Katrina struck managed to reopen his school two months after the storm. He received widespread acclaim for getting the school repaired following the hurricane. McGinn stepped down from his post in 2011 after about two decades in the role, taking over the job of assistant for secondary education with the New Orleans Province of the Jesuits. However, he reassumed the Jesuit presidency in 2014 on an interim basis after his successor, Father Raymond Fitzgerald, was diagnosed with the neuromuscular disease commonly referred to as ALS. McGinn once again earned praise for coming forward to lead Jesuit at a time when it was needed by the school, when students and alums were shaken by the news affecting Fitzgerald, a popular priest and educator in his own right. McGinn was slated to turn over the reins to a new Jesuit president—Father Christopher Scott Fronk, a U.S. Navy commander and chaplain—in November 2016.

Doug Thornton: Now Executive Vice President for SMG, Thornton oversees the company's Stadium and Arena operations throughout the country, including the Superdome and the next-door arena now known as the Smoothie King Center. Since Katrina, those buildings have hosted a

Super Bowl, two college-football national championship games, two NBA All-Star contests, both the NCAA Men's and Women's Final Four and Wrestlemania XXX, among other events.

Adrianne LeBlanc: Adrianne, along with assistant principal, Sister Marie Jo, remains the principal of St. Dominic in Lakeview. Before the storm, approximately seven hundred students were enrolled in the school. After the storm, one hundred students initially enrolled at the satellite campus at Holy Rosary. Since then, the school's enrollment at the Lakeview campus has swelled to five hundred ninety-nine students from among four hundred eleven families.

William Herrington, Jr: After graduating from Belmont University in Nashville in 2009, our oldest son, William, moved to Los Angeles, where he earned a Masters in Jazz Piano from the University of Southern California. He is now a professional studio and touring keyboardist for various pop artists. He released his first solo album, *Solace,* in April, 2015, paying tribute to his beloved hometown of New Orleans.

Katherine Herrington: Our daughter, Katherine, graduated from Second Baptist High School in Houston, the school led by Pastor Ed Young, who organized "Operation Compassion" after Hurricane Katrina to aid storm victims. She is now attending the University of Texas. While she still owns and cherishes the pink phone her mother and I salvaged from our flooded home in Metairie shortly after Katrina, she uses a cell phone these days—a lot, I might add.

Chris Herrington: Our son, Chris, finished his eighth grade year in May 2006 at New Orleans Jesuit. He was the only "platooned" Strake Jesuit eighth grader to then enroll at

Strake Jesuit for the ninth grade after we permanently moved to Houston in June 2006. In his junior year at Strake Jesuit, Chris was presented with the Crusader award, which is annually presented to "that student or students who, in the eyes of the faculty, responded to, and most benefitted from, the influence of the Strake Jesuit Community environment." Chris later graduated from Strake Jesuit in 2010, tying for second-highest academic honors. His Strake Jesuit education proved worthwhile—he went on to graduate with high honors in petroleum engineering from the University of Texas. Now working in Houston, Chris and several of his 2005 classmates, including Kevin Lafferty, Bucky Ribbeck, and Joe Higgs, occasionally attend charity events at Strake Jesuit in the name of the 2010 graduating class.

Mr. Harrigan: Born Edward Joseph and nicknamed "E.J.," like our insurance agent friend from the boat rescue after the storm, Mr. Harrigan died on August 19, 2010, at the age of 89. During my research, I came across his obituary and learned that he had some things in common with my family. For instance, he graduated from Jesuit High School in New Orleans in 1938. His wife's name was Frances, like mine. And his late father's first name and middle initial were the same as mine, "William P." According to his obituary, which ran in *The Times-Picayune,* Mr. Harrigan was a chief petty officer for the U.S. Navy during World II before joining the Coast Guard. He was a member of the Veterans of Foreign Wars Post No. 6640, and he owned and operated a refrigeration service. He and his late wife had three children and five grandchildren.

Frances and Bill: Frances now works part-time and volunteers at St. Michael Catholic School in Houston, a job very similar to the position she had at St. Dominic in

New Orleans. As for me, I am a corporate banker with Capital One. Until just recently, I've maintained an office just outside that fishbowl on the sixth floor, where many of my New Orleans colleagues and I set up a temporary office after the storm as we tried our best to get our bank and customers back on their feet. This bank office recently relocated to another Capital One building just up the street, on Westheimer Boulevard in Houston and my office was moved to downtown Houston.

Frances and I continue to be interested and involved in education.

Before I let you go, allow me to say one more thing.

Who dat!

BIBLIOGRAPHY

Arrupe, Pedro, S.J. "Men For Others. Education for social justice and social action today." 1973, accessed on April 5, 2016: http://onlineministries.creighton.edu/CollaborativeMinistry/men-for-others.html.

Barry, John M. *Rising Tide: The Great Mississippi Flood of 1927 and How It Changed America.* New York: Simon and Schuster, 1997.

Bea, Robert G. "Failure of the New Orleans 17th Street Canal Levee & Floodwall During Hurricane Katrina." GeoCongress (March 9-12, 2008): doi: 10.1061/40962(325)23.

Bezou, Henry. *Metairie: A Tongue of Land to Pasture.* Louisiana: Pelican Publishing, 1973.

Brunkard, Joan, Gonza Namulanda, and Raoult Ratard. "Hurricane Katrina Deaths Louisiana, 2005." American Medical Association and Lippincott, Williams and Wilkins (August 2008): doi: 10.1097.

"Chapter Four: History of the New Orleans Flood Protection System." Independent Levee Investigation Team. New Orleans Levee Systems, Hurricane Katrina, July 31, 2006.

Culberson, John. "Tribute to Harris County Judge Robert Eckels," Capitol Words, last modified March 14, 2007: http://capitolwords.org/date/2007/03/14/E540-2_tribute-to-harris-county-judge-robert-eckels.

Hearing On Recovering From Hurricane Katrina: Responding to the Needs of the Displaced, Today And Tomorrow, Before the Senate Homeland Security and Governmental Affairs Committee, 109th Cong. (2005) (statement of Robert A. Eckels, County Judge, Harris County, Texas).

Hibernia Corporation, *1994 Annual Report.*

Hoadley, Russ. "A Beacon of Hope: Hibernia Bank's recovery from Hurricane Katrina." August 9, 2015: http://hiberniakatrina.com.

"Houston's Helping Hand: Remembering Katrina," *Houston History* 7, no. 3 (Summer 2010), http://houstonhistorymagazine.org/pdfs/v7n3.pdf. The interviews and photographs used in the issue are housed in the Houston History Archives, Special Collections, University of Houston Libraries.

Katz, Bruce and Jennifer Bradley. *The Metropolitan Revolution: How Cities and Metros Are Fixing Our Broken Politics And Fragile Economy.* Washington: Brookings Institution Press, 2013.

Klineberg, Stephen. "Four Myths About Katrina's Impact on Houston." Urban Edge, Kinder Institute, August 26, 2015: http://urbanedge.blogs. rice.edu/2015/08/26/four-myths-about-katrinas-impact-on-houston/#. VwrLpzP2ZD9.

"Lakeview, New Orleans." Wikipedia. The Wikipedia Foundation, last modified March 7, 2016: https://en.wikipedia.org/wiki/Lakeview,_New_ Orleans. Much of the data about Lakeview was derived from this source.

LeBlanc, Adrianne, to the parents, students, and/or staff at St. Dominic School. October 3 and 16, 2005; November 27, 2005; May 2006.

Loudenback, Doug. "A Hornets Oklahoma City Reader: The Hornets, Oklahoma City, New Orleans, and the Media 2005-2006." Doug Louden-back on the Web, last accessed April 14, 2016. Various statistics related to the Hornets were derived from this source.

Marshall, Bob. "New Orleanians gradually accepting radical new attitude toward water." The Advocate, last modified March 2, 2015: http:// redevelop.nola.gov/news/headlines/198-new-orleanians-gradually-ac-cept-radical-new-attitude-toward-water.

Mealer, Bryan. "The Power of Government to Do Good; Citizen of the Year," *Esquire Magazine,* November 30, 2005.

Nelson, Stephen A., "Why New Orleans is Vulnerable to Hurricanes. Geologic and Historical Factors." Tulane University, last modified December 10, 2012: http://www.tulane.edu/~sanelson/New_Orleans_ and_Hurricanes/New_Orleans_Vulnerability.htm.

O'Connell, Kim. "Shelter From the Storms." American City and County, last modified July 1, 2006: http://americancityandcounty.com/features/ government_shelter_storms.

Rogers, J.D. "Development of the New Orleans Flood Protection System prior to Hurricane Katrina." *Journal of Geotechnical and Geoenviron-mental Engineering,* ASCE, May, 2008.

Smith, Jimmy. "Pelicans, Hornets and Thunder owe NBA existence to George Shinn." *Times Picayune,* November 3, 2014.

Taggart, Chuck. "A lexicon of New Orleans Terminology and Speech: How ta tawk rite." The Gumbo Pages, last accessed April 5, 2016: www. gumbopages.com/yatspeak.

"Through the Eye of Katrina: The Past as Prologue?" *The Journal of American History* 94 (December 2007): 693-876.

INDEX

ABOUT THE AUTHOR

As a corporate banker in New Orleans for 20 years, Bill Herrington actively supported community education alongside his wife Frances, a teacher. He uses his unique perspective of the extraordinary leadership witnessed after Katrina to raise funds to support the education of youth who are impacted by natural disasters or family tragedies.

Please consider contributing to institutions that provide educational resources and support for students in need. If none come to mind, I've listed a few below that I believe are worthy of your support:

Strake Jesuit College Preparatory, Houston, Texas
www.strakejesuit.org

Jesuit High School, New Orleans, Louisiana
www.jesuitnola.org

St. Cecilia Catholic School, Houston, Texas
www.saintceciliacatholicschool.org

Regis High School, New York, New York
www.regis.org

YES Prep Public Schools, Houston, Texas
www.yesprep.org

St. Dominic School, New Orleans, Louisiana
www.stdominicnola.org/st-dominic-church

St. Michael Catholic School, Houston, Texas
www.stmichaelcs.org

San Francisco Nativity Academy, Houston, Texas
www.nativityhouston.org

Neighborhood Centers, Inc., Houston, Texas
www.neighborhood-centers.org

Cristo Rey Jesuit College Preparatory of Houston
www.cristoreyjesuit.org